# JUSTICE IN A GLOBAL ECONOMY

# JUSTICE IN A GLOBAL ECONOMY

## Strategies for Home, Community, and World

*Pamela K. Brubaker*
*Rebecca Todd Peters*
*Laura A. Stivers*
Editors

Westminster John Knox Press
LOUISVILLE • LONDON

*Book design by Sharon Adams*
*Cover design by Eric Walljasper, Minneapolis, MN*

*First edition*
Published by Westminster John Knox Press
Louisville, Kentucky

This book is printed on acid-free paper that meets the American National Standards Institute Z39.48 standard.⊗

PRINTED IN THE UNITED STATES OF AMERICA

06 07 08 09 10 11 12 13 14 15 — 10 9 8 7 6 5 4 3 2 1

Library of Congress Cataloging-in-Publication Data is on file at the Library of Congress, Washington, D.C.

ISBN-13: 978-0-664-22955-9

ISBN-10: 0-664-22955-7

# Contents

Contributors                                                                 vii

Introduction                                                                   1

**Part One. Household Strategies**

  1. Supporting Community Farming by Rebecca Todd Peters              17

  2. Relating to Household Labor Justly by W. Anne Joh                29

  3. Consuming Responsibly by Marcia Allen Owens                      40

  4. Eating Intentionally by Shannon Jung                             50

**Part Two. Community Strategies**

  5. Holding Corporations Accountable by Laura Stivers                65

  6. Engaging Environmental Justice by Carlton Waterhouse             78

  7. Revitalizing Local Communities by Wylin Dassie                  91

  8. Creating the Commons by Larry L. Rasmussen                     101

**Part Three. Public Policy Strategies**

  9. Promoting Solidarity with Migrants by Daisy L. Machado         115

  10. Reforming Global Economic Policies by Pamela K. Brubaker      127

  11. Ensuring Sustainability by John B. Cobb Jr.                   140

  12. Challenging Our Assumptions by Mary Elizabeth Hobgood         150

Index                                                                       161

# Contributors

**Pamela K. Brubaker** is Professor of Religion at California Lutheran University. Her most recent book is *Globalization at What Price? Economic Change and Daily Life* (Pilgrim Press, 2001). She serves on the board of the Society of Christian Ethics and is cochair of the Sweatshop Action and Worker Justice Committee of Progressive Christians Uniting in Los Angeles.

**John B. Cobb Jr.** is Professor of Theology Emeritus at Claremont Theological School. He is the author of the Grawemeyer Award–winning book *For the Common Good: Redirecting the Economy Toward Community, the Environment, and a Sustainable Future,* with Herman Daly (Beacon Press, 1994). He is a codirector of the Center for Process Studies in Claremont, California, and a cofounder of Progressive Christians Uniting. Cobb is an ordained minister in the United Methodist Church.

**Wylin Dassie** is a doctoral student in the Graduate Division of Religion at Emory University, Georgia. Her publications include "A Microenterprise-Centered Economic Development Strategy for the Rural South: Sustaining Growth with Economic Opportunity," with Ralph D. Christy and Mark D. Wenner, in the *Journal of Agricultural and Applied Economics.* She serves as a member of the Emerging Markets Program Advisory Board at Cornell University.

**Mary Elizabeth Hobgood** is Associate Professor of Religious Studies at Holy Cross College, Massachusetts. Her most recent book is *Dismantling Privilege: An Ethics of Accountability* (Pilgrim Press, 2000). Hobgood has been a faculty contributor to Seminary Summer of the Interfaith Committee on Worker Justice.

**W. Anne Joh** is Assistant Professor of Theology at Phillips Theological Seminary in Oklahoma. She has published *Heart of the Cross: A Postcolonial Christology* (Louisville: Westminster John Knox Press, 2006). Joh is a lay leader in the United Methodist Church and a member of the Work Group for Constructive Theology.

**Shannon Jung** is Professor of Town and Country Ministries at Saint Paul School of Theology in Kansas City. For a number of years he directed the Center for Theology and Land at Wartburg and the University of Dubuque seminaries. He is the author of *Food for Life: The Spirituality and Ethics of Eating* (Augsburg Fortress, 2004). Jung is an ordained Presbyterian Church (U.S.A.) minister.

**Daisy L. Machado** is currently Dean of the Lexington Theological Seminary. Previously she was Associate Professor of History of Christianity and Hispanic Church Studies at Brite Divinity School. Among her publications is "The Unnamed Woman: Justice, Feminists, and the Undocumented Woman" in *A Reader in Latina Feminist Theology: Religion and Justice,* edited by María Pilar Aquino, Daisy L. Machado, and Jeanette Rodríguez (University of Texas Press, 2002). She has been taking seminary students to the border for over ten years. Machado is an ordained minister of the Christian Church (Disciples of Christ), the first Latina ordained in the United States.

**Marcia Allen Owens** is an environmental lawyer, Director of the FAMU Teaching Learning Institute, and a member of the faculty of the Environmental Sciences Institute at Florida A&M University. Owens also served as a Lilly Postdoctoral Fellow in Religious Practices and Practical Theology at the Candler School of Theology at Emory University. Owens is an ordained elder in the African Methodist Episcopal Church.

**Rebecca Todd Peters** is Distinguished Emerging Scholar and Assistant Professor of Religious Studies at Elon University, North Carolina. She is the author of *In Search of the Good Life: The Ethics of Globalization* (Continuum, 2004), winner of the 2003 Trinity Prize. She has been active in young women's leadership development through the Presbyterian Church (U.S.A.), the National Council of Churches, and the World Council of Churches. She is an ordained Presbyterian Church (U.S.A.) minister.

**Larry Rasmussen** is the Reinhold Niebuhr Professor of Social Ethics Emeritus at Union Theological Seminary in New York. He is the author of the Grawemeyer Award–winning book *Earth Ethics, Earth Community* (Orbis Books, 1996). He served as co-moderator of the Unit III, Justice, Peace, Creation of the World Council of Churches.

**Laura Stivers** is Associate Professor of Philosophy and Religion at Pfeiffer University, North Carolina. Among her publications is "Resistance to Structural Adjustment Policies" in *Resistance and Theological Ethics,* edited by Robert L. Stivers and Ronald H. Stone (Rowman & Littlefield Publishers, 2004). She has been active in popular economic education through the grassroots group Just Economics.

**Carlton Waterhouse** is Assistant Professor of Law at the Florida International University College of Law as well as a doctoral candidate in Ethics in the Graduate Division of Religion at Emory University. His professional legal experience includes ten years of service as an attorney for the Environmental Protection Agency where he assisted in the development of the agency's environmental justice policies.

# Introduction

*Pamela K. Brubaker, Rebecca Todd Peters, and Laura Stivers*

Your well-paying computer job has been outsourced to India; you are unable to pay your health insurance premiums; you discover that 80 percent of the food you eat is genetically modified, that all of your elected politicians are millionaires, and that corporate advertising is inundating your kids' schools. As an American you might have experienced one or all of these negative effects of economic globalization. The situation is considerably worse for two-thirds of the people in the world, many of whom have been uprooted from their land to make way for agribusinesses only to suffer unemployment in overcrowded cities. Many people in our world lack basic necessities such as suitable housing, clean water, food, health care, and education. Although poverty is an age-old problem, in many places economic globalization has exacerbated, not alleviated, it.

Most of us would agree that these negative effects of economic globalization do not coincide with our visions of a healthy society. We have a sense of dis-ease, but we often feel overwhelmed by the seeming inevitability of economic globalization and rising corporate power. We wonder what we as individuals or even as communities can do. In addition, we sometimes have ambivalence about globalization. Despite its drawbacks, many Americans experience some benefit from an economic system that rewards those who have disposable income. We have access to any type of food we want, any time of year; we can communicate instantaneously with people around the globe and readily travel to any destination we desire; we can buy electronics and clothes and many other consumer goods quite cheaply. What we have not quite gotten around to examining are the ethics that underlie decisions we make about how we spend our money, where we work, how we invest, what we do with our "free" time, and many other aspects of daily life.

We, the editors of this volume, are three white women who are active in Christian churches and social justice movements that seek to challenge and problematize preconceived ideas about the inevitability and beneficence of economic globalization. We are all professors of social ethics who are passionately committed to teaching and activism that promote God's vision of *ekklēsia* or a community of equals. We believe that those of us "at the top," who do benefit in some ways from economic globalization, bear some responsibility for the negative implications of our lifestyles on those "at the bottom." In compiling this volume we invited a diverse group of contributors to help us reflect on these responsibilities.

This desire to question our behavior and complicity in the increasing destitution of the majority of the world's people is not intended to elicit guilt among our readers—indeed, quite the contrary. Guilt is often accompanied by social paralysis. To avoid feeling guilty, many of us simply avoid situations that might prompt guilt. In other words, if we feel guilty when we think about the ways in which our lifestyles are bought at the price of the sacrifice of others, the easiest solution is simply not to think about our actions at all. Life is much simpler this way. After all, most of us have enough trouble getting dinner on the table for our families without trying to figure out how far the food traveled to get there or how much the workers who harvested the crops were paid.

Unfortunately, sticking our heads in the sand does not absolve us of our responsibility to our neighbor. As Jesus taught in the parable of the Good Samaritan, we are responsible to care for our neighbors—even when we do not know them. We cannot allow our guilt to paralyze us into inaction. Guilt has no place in Christian community. Christ did not come to make us feel guilty, but to teach us a new way to live. Christ's vision of a better world includes a profound message of forgiveness that allows us to continue to function in the world. Many of us buy clothes made in sweatshops, drive SUVs, or eat food grown in unsustainable ways. This is often a result of how unreflective Americans are about our consumer behaviors. Most of us are ignorant of many of the ethical problems associated with our consumer behaviors. Perhaps others of us feel powerless to live our lives in alternative ways that challenge the status quo. Either way, we end up contributing to the problems of economic injustice and environmental degradation in our world.

While Christ teaches us that forgiveness is indeed a free gift from God, it is not intended to be a free pass for living an unreflective life. In a world of social injustice and ecological destruction, it is not enough to live our lives simply being nice to others, refraining from lying, cheating, and stealing, and basking in God's love and blessing. We are called to reflect on the blessings in our lives and to examine how our lives are interconnected with millions of people around the world *whom we will never know*. Where have our blessings come from? Are there structures and powers that exist in the world that have contributed to our affluence, our well-being, what we might call our "blessedness"? We are called to respond to God's desire for the well-being of the whole creation by taking responsibility for our lives and the ways in which we help and hurt others— intentionally or unintentionally.

We are indeed freed by God's forgiveness, but we are freed for a new life in Christ that requires us to live differently, a new life that asks us to participate in building God's vision of a new heaven and a new earth. Each of us is called to follow Christ in working to build God's kin-dom[1] here on earth, and Jesus' actions and ministry offer us a guide to follow. Just as he ministered to the sick, the poor, the outcast, and the needy, we are called to look into the faces of our neighbors and respond. Jesus lived his life in opposition to the dominant powers of his world in an effort to help others and to transform the world around him. Following Jesus' call, we seek a society in which preventable social problems like hunger, illiteracy, abuse, and child labor become a historical memory rather than a present reality.

Our hope for this book is that it will motivate people to make changes in their own lifestyles and to organize with others to change institutions and policies so that all inhabitants of the earth as well as the earth itself can, as theologian Sallie McFague says, "live abundantly." The abundant life will be based "not on material goods, but on those things that really make people happy: the basic necessities of food, clothing, and shelter for themselves and their children; medical care and educational opportunities; loving relationships; meaningful work; an enriching imaginative and spiritual life; and time spent with friends and in the natural world."[2]

Many books analyze what globalization is and how it affects us, but not very many offer concrete suggestions for how to respond to it.[3] In this book we start from the assumption that economic globalization, in its present form, is causing more harm than good. Although this is a contested assumption, the goal of this book is not to convince readers that economic globalization is causing harm. We write to those who are already aware of its negative effects, either directly or indirectly, and want to know what they can do to make our economic systems more socially and environmentally just. We think this book is unique for two reasons. One, we offer strategies for resisting the current model of economic globalization and for rethinking how we can promote just and sustainable communities. Two, we do our rethinking from within a Christian ethical framework for those who connect such resistance to faith and spirituality.

## UNDERSTANDING THE CURRENT PROBLEM

Since the fall of the Berlin Wall in 1989 and the virtual disappearance of state-sponsored communism, capitalism has risen to the fore as the reigning economic model. There are few places in the world where nation-states are experimenting with economic models other than the capitalist model. While China has certainly retained a strong state-centered political economy, it has eagerly embraced capitalism and economic growth as the Chinese seek to become more respected participants in the global economy. It is true that capitalist countries have evidenced stronger support for the democratic freedoms and values that most of us in North America cherish and desire. Nevertheless, an uncritical valorization of capitalism as synonymous with democracy and freedom can allow us to overlook some of the deep ethical problems that are also associated with the model of capitalism that marks our current era.[4]

New strategies for promoting free-market capitalism and economic integration focus on three primary public policy strategies—privatization, deregulation, and liberalization of trade and finance. Privatization is the move to place assets and services that have traditionally been owned and managed by the government into the hands of private business. Transportation, education, prison systems, and the postal service are examples of services that have historically been managed by state and federal governments in the United States. It has traditionally been part of our philosophy that certain tasks and services are so important for the common good of the community, especially those to which all citizens should have access, that they should be managed by the government. When goods are in the private sector, we have less say about who will have access to them. "Deregulation" refers to the attempt to get rid of governmental regulations that affect the business community. Proponents argue that regulations hamper the efficiency of the market and get in the way of a "free market." Since the 1980s, numerous regulations intended to protect consumer safety, the environment, and worker safety have been struck down as impediments to the market. Finally, reigning economic theory is oriented toward increasing the volume of international trade. This is often accomplished through "free" trade agreements that remove or reduce tariffs or quotas on goods and services and restrictions on foreign investment. Although in principle this may seem reasonable, in a world with huge imbalances of power, wealth, and capacity, the results are mixed. For example, the North American Free Trade Agreement (NAFTA) has led to job losses in both the United States and Mexico. The net loss of U.S. manufacturing jobs is roughly 1 million while the agricultural sector in Mexico is estimated to have lost 1.3 million jobs.[5]

We are certainly not rejecting all international trade or market economies. Our strategies focus on resisting the current model of economic globalization known as "neoliberalism." This model promotes the free market as the best route to ensuring economic development and political, economic, moral, and cultural liberty. More specifically, it aims for freer international trade and investment, less social and environmental regulations for corporations, the privatization of state-owned enterprises, and a decrease in social spending. Proponents believe that a market free of government regulation and intervention will promote the most economic growth, which will in turn benefit the most people. We argue that the neoliberal economic model has been detrimental to most people and to the environment. We will highlight just a few of the problems associated with the current economic model.

Global financial institutions like the International Monetary Fund (IMF), the World Bank, and the World Trade Organization (WTO) have acquired such power and status in our global economy that they are able to pressure countries into implementing neoliberal economic policies as prerequisites for participation in the global marketplace. Countries needing loans to pay off debt must agree to structural adjustment programs, in effect restructuring their economies to fit the neoliberal policy agenda. Even recent concessions of debt forgiveness orchestrated by the G-8 (Group of 8: United States, Great Britain, Canada, Italy, France, Germany, Japan, and Russia) in Scotland were tied to neoliberal market reforms. Proponents of this economic model argue that handing over economic decision making from the state to the free market is an inevitable process that is the result of large historical factors. While they acknowledge that countries narrow their political and economic policy choices by adopting a free-market-oriented economic agenda, they argue that the increased economic growth and prosperity is worth it. One of the most dangerous side effects of current market reforms, however, is the emphasis on reducing social spending, which has made education and health care less accessible for many people in the world. The emphasis on privatization of state-owned enterprises has also led to the provision of fewer public goods and services. The private sector does not need to ensure accessibility to goods and often charges more than many people can pay. The privatization of water in Bolivia, where rates tripled or even quadrupled, is a good example.[6]

In light of the growing inequality between the rich and poor around the world in recent decades, we question the faith that has been placed in this "one model fits all" approach to economic activity and the promise of prosperity that underlies it. Indeed, the current model of economic globalization has led to greater inequality.[7] Critics call it the "20:80 Society," wherein the top 20 percent of the population participate in the life, earnings, and consumption of the system, while the other 80 percent are exploited or, even worse, marginalized by the system.[8] By 2003 the compensation for CEOs in the United States was estimated to be 301 times the average worker's pay, up from 42 times the average worker's pay in 1980.[9] According to United for a Fair Economy, changes in family income in the United States from 1947 to 1979 were roughly equal across the economic spectrum, with incomes in the bottom 20 percent rising slightly faster than those in the top 20 percent. This shifted dramatically from 1979 to 2001, the period that coincides with the rise of neoliberal economic policies, when incomes in the bottom 20 percent of the population rose by only 3 percent, while the top 20 percent rose by 53 percent and the top 5 percent by 81 percent.[10] Global inequalities also increased in this period. The United Nations' *Human Development Report 1999* reported that "the gap in per capita income (GNP) between the countries with the richest fifth of the world's people and those with the poorest fifth widened from 30 to 1 in 1960, to 60 to 1 in 1990, to 74 to 1 in 1995."[11] Statistics for inequality in the distribution of wealth rather than income would show even greater disparity both nationally and globally.

In addition to questions about the current model's ability to promote economic benefits for the most marginalized citizens of our world, there are also questions about this model's impact on our environment. The decrease in governmental regulations on environmental issues has led to increased environmental destruction.[12] Furthermore, the economic development strategies promoted by structural adjustment policies are not environmentally friendly. For example, many countries are forced to switch from small-scale sustainable agriculture to large-scale industrial export agriculture to bring in money for debt interest payments.

The current economic model also privileges an individualistic approach to decision making that assumes people make "rational" economic decisions that promote their own self-interest. This assumption that individuals are selfish and indifferent to how others fare leads to policies with thin notions of relationship or the common good. While economists have long claimed that economics is a value-neutral "science," this focus on individual well-being as a core element of the framework of free-market capitalism functions to hinder it from promoting economic activity that reflects just social relations.

Furthermore, there are values that serve to channel and direct current models of economic activity. Recent economic restructuring that lessens governmental involvement and seeks to promote maximum profit gives preference to the values of profit and efficiency over other values like sustainability and economic justice. This restructuring encourages corporations to maximize their profits. The argument is that corporate profit will lead to more jobs. Often the opposite occurs—workers are deemed "inefficient" and replaced by machines. Moreover, a large amount of profit being made in the global economy is not from productive investment, but from extractive investment in the form of financial speculation. This is nothing more than sophisticated gambling and does nothing to create jobs or wealth for communities. Simply put, when economies are structured primarily around profit, the interests of money will be more important than the interests of people or the environment.

The current model of economic globalization is not concerned about meaningful work that is geographically and environmentally sensitive to particular communities. Corporations prioritizing profit seek to shed labor and environmental standards and are not particularly concerned about creating enough work for all, let alone meaningful work. Indeed, given the internal logic of the system to keep wages low, it is in their best interest to have a pool of unemployed people seeking work. Economic globalization is displacing more and more people as well. These displaced people often become a cheap and flexible labor force in the globalized economy.

Proponents of neoliberal economic globalization argue that it encourages democracy because financial investors want to invest only in countries that are stable and have open and clear economic and political procedures. Critics argue that what is democracy in name is in truth "plutocracy" in which the monied interests of a few have inordinate power. Of the largest one hundred economies in the world today, fifty-one are corporations. Between corporate power, trade agreements such as NAFTA and CAFTA, and international financial institutions such as the IMF, World Bank, and the WTO (none of which is democratic), the power and autonomy of national, state, and local governments to govern their own economies has been restricted. The interests of international trade, which coincide with the interests of transnational corporations, take precedence. For example, international organizations have increasingly restricted governments from instituting environmental and social protections.

## CREATING JUST HOUSEHOLDS, COMMUNITIES, AND ENVIRONMENTS

Because our goal is to be more constructive than critical, we offer a general vision of characteristics that we think just societies exhibit. We are not trying to offer a one-size-fits-all blueprint for how communities should be organized. In fact, we believe there are and should be a plurality of models for just and healthy community. Within this plurality, however, there are common elements. One is what we call narrow inequality. Just societies are not likely to have complete equality since there will always be differences in talent and motivation, but they will have public policies that sharply narrow the gap in wealth and income. For example, there might be safety nets put in place so that no one goes below a certain standard of living, and there might be a maximum wage law as well as progressive taxation.

Another common element of just societies is the commitment to sustainability. Justice requires that healthy households and communities will respect the earth and its living inhabitants and find ways to live within the limits of the earth's carrying capacity, or what the earth is able to sustain. In today's world, economic growth is valued over sustainability. Societies oriented toward justice will require a different economic system than unbridled capitalism.

Technology, industry, and agriculture would be modeled on sustainability, and the use of renewable resources would be the norm. Lastly, households would take seriously population control and sustainable consumption.

Just societies will also have a commitment to healthy relationships in and between communities. Just societies view individuals as social by nature, but are also aware of the oppressive ways that humans can relate. Such societies will have public policies that respect individual rights, yet also view individuals as part of larger families and groups. These policies would protect both individuals and groups from various oppressions (e.g., racism, sexism) as well as proactively resist oppression. In a just society, profit and efficiency would not take precedence over all other values. Resources would be invested in creating healthy communities and environments where caring relationships can develop. The end goal of any economic and political system would be the flourishing of God's creation. The interests of people and the environment would be given more priority than the interests of money.

Work and productivity are also necessary for a just society, but not simply as a means to profit. A healthy society will find ways to make more work fulfilling and will ensure that work environments are safe and support human dignity. A just society will also find ways to promote local development that provides meaningful jobs that pay a living wage for people in their geographical environment so that they can have roots in a place—a home. Local development will fit the needs of the community and be environmentally sensitive.

For communities to be able to address their particular social and environmental needs, the principle of subsidiarity will be important. That is, decisions will be made at the most local level possible. National policies will still be important to ensure standards of social and environmental justice and to regulate fairness between communities, but a majority of power would be decentralized so that people can participate in defining their own development. Most importantly, local and national politics will not be dominated by big-money interests. A just society will have a democracy where votes count and leaders get elected according to what policies they support, not according to how deep their pockets are.

Lastly, just societies will value good education and health care for all. Policies will ensure accessibility and not restrict such important goods to those who can pay. Public goods that are paid for by tax money will be given importance. Just societies will also be organized around patterns of work, family, and relaxation that allow for families and communities to care for one another. Active concern for the development and well-being of children will go far beyond providing quality education to all, but will also include quality day care, after school care, and elder care as well as programs that facilitate the development of relationships of mentoring and care for children at risk. Recognition of our common humanity and responsibility to care for one another as sisters and brothers will replace society's current overemphasis on individualism.

## STRATEGIES FOR PROMOTING JUST
## AND HEALTHY SOCIETIES

Clearly there is much work to be done if we hope to transform globalization into a more just and healthy model for social interaction. In working, teaching, organizing, and talking with people across the United States, we repeatedly encounter a certain sense of hopelessness among students, laypeople, and concerned citizens alike. This hopelessness is rooted in a despairing sense of the massive scale of the problems that are associated with the current form of economic globalization and an inability to see how we might begin to work together to effect change in these global systems of oppression and domination. Many people agree that something is wrong, but they simply do not know what to do about it.

We have written this book to help individuals and their communities begin to see ways that they can facilitate the necessary transformation toward justice in which our faith calls us to participate. We have hope for a better future, hope for a world community that approximates justice, and hope for a healthier planet and human community. Some people call us and our vision naive; we prefer to think of ourselves as followers of Christ who are called to justice. We believe that our purpose in life is to work toward making the world more just. We are quite cognizant of the powers that be and how they are arrayed against our vision of hope and transformation. In the chapters that follow you will read critical assessments of the current political-economic structures that dominate our world, but with those assessments come examples of people and communities who are actively involved in making a new way. We hope that these chapters will encourage you to organize your household toward personal lifestyle changes and inspire your church or civic organization to take up community and public policy work to transform the status quo.

The book is divided into three parts—household, community, and public policy—because these are the three arenas where social change occurs. While many of the issues and problems raised in these chapters can (and should) be addressed on the individual, community, and public policy level, we have asked each author to focus on one particular level for ease of comprehension and activism. We believe that ultimately it is essential for change to take place on all three levels simultaneously in order for larger-scale transformation to take place.

If you are new to these issues and feel overwhelmed by the magnitude of the problems, we encourage you to start small, to set a goal to work toward for three to six months. As we hope you will see by the end of this book, much of the problem that we face is ideological—our ideas about what is possible have been shaped and formed by the prevailing economic logic of neoliberal capitalism in ways that often disallow alternative visions of how we might order our society and our economy. By making small steps in our personal lifestyles we can begin to challenge the dominant ideology that sometimes shapes our vision of the future. As our habits and practices begin to change, our minds often become more open to new possibilities for the future.

It is often easiest to begin projects on a small scale, such as by joining a CSA (Community Supported Agriculture) farm, starting a compost pile, or renegotiating our relationship with people who work in our homes (e.g., housecleaning, child care, lawn service). Making changes in our own households is often the most manageable place to begin. Furthermore, it is hard to convince others of the need for change if we have not addressed our own complicity in undermining healthy societies. Taking one step at a time is key. That said, we do not have to have a spotless individual record (buy exclusively organic food, have all of our assets in socially responsible funds, etc.) before we can begin to work with others resisting the current form of economic globalization. Similarly, policies aimed at a healthy society will not be instituted at the national level unless there is enough household and community support for them.

We hope that this book can be a guide for thinking about the ethical and spiritual issues at stake as well as offering suggestions for how your church; PTA; women's group, men's group, or youth group; or Sunday school class might begin to organize around larger community and public policy strategies that will change the face of your town or local community as well as change the face of globalization on a larger scale. While you might want to try to follow some of the suggestions or examples illustrated in these chapters, they can also serve as a stimulus for creative thinking about what the most pressing problems are in your community and how you might work with others to develop strategies for addressing the problems. We have included discussion questions at the end of each chapter to prompt such thinking and strategizing.

Households are the focus of the first section of the book, with chapters that describe individual strategies and practices that we can do on an individual basis within our families. Rebecca Todd Peters looks at how households can support local economies and environmentally healthy food production through Community Supported Agriculture. She compares corporate agribusiness with biodynamic and organic farming, arguing that the latter promotes the long-term thriving of the earth and people. Furthermore, she argues that a relational connection to farmers and the earth can serve an important role in moral formation. Discussion questions highlight the relationship between eating and food production and prompt us to think about our own moral agency in relation to the food we eat.

Anne Joh examines how those of us who employ household labor can do so justly. She examines experiences of domestic laborers in the current global economic order—experiences that cause "bruised hearts." While not ignoring power discrepancies, she proposes labor relationships based on reciprocity, interdependence, and mutuality, drawing on Christian and Korean traditions that speak to a "fullness of the heart." Discussion questions prompt readers to identify injustices in caregiving work and envision ways to revalue and relate to household labor justly.

Marcia Owens considers the excessive consumption patterns of Americans that have become a virus (affluenza), infecting individual households as well as churches. She argues that we need to come to a new awareness, giving priority to the norms of sustainability and sufficiency. To lead us to such an awareness, she offers questions that help assess our consumption, and examples of how churches have become more environmentally and socially responsible in their behaviors and practices. Discussion questions prompt awareness of our purchasing patterns and ways to be responsible consumers.

Shannon Jung concludes this section by analyzing the quality, safety, and availability of food in the current system of economic globalization and our spending and eating practices in the affluent world. He gives strategies for implementing a Christian vision of good eating based on honoring our bodies through delight and sharing, promoting more equitable distribution of the costs of food production and eating, and promoting more environmentally sustainable food production. Discussion questions prompt reflection on how cultural forces of global capitalism affect the way we eat and envision a spirituality of eating based on delight, sharing, and treating all bodies as temples.

Communities are the focus of the second section of the book, with chapters that describe what communities and congregations are doing to address problems resulting from economic globalization. Laura Stivers considers the community impact of job displacement caused by "footloose capital." She looks to the community benefit agreement negotiated by a broad-based coalition of organizations in Los Angeles for lessons in how to hold corporations accountable to local communities. She argues for an alternative vision of economic globalization based on protection of the common good and rootedness to particular places. Discussion questions challenge communities and congregations to address issues of job quality and local corporate accountability standards as a way to promote the common good.

Carlton Waterhouse analyzes the connections between globalization and environmental injustice. He tells the inspiring story of ReGenesis, a South Carolina community organization that successfully transformed a distressed neighborhood. He argues that their success was due to communally negotiated and shared virtues that guided them in developing effective strategies and approaches to environmental injustices. These communal virtues sustained the community, allowed them to weather adversities, and inspired hope in other communities. Discussion questions promote awareness of environmental injustice and ways that communities and congregations can foster communal virtues in addressing problems posed by economic globalization.

Wylin Dassie examines how congregations, following the biblical mandate of concern for the poor and needy, have been reevaluating their public role in response to changes wrought by economic globalization. She illustrates different

ways that congregations have participated in community economic development strategies and addresses the difficulty of securing funding for such efforts.
Discussion questions ask congregations to identify ministry projects that
address local needs and challenge them to think theologically about community responsibility.

Larry Rasmussen argues that creation is a commons to which we all belong
and gives five examples of communities that are re-creating the commons, from
land trusts in the United States to African "Earthkeeping" Churches. All of
these examples honor the land and the local community as the commons, a
value that economic globalization does not take seriously. Discussion questions
rekindle a sense of belonging to the land and encourage readers to envision ways
that communities and congregations can create the commons.

Public policies, particularly those of the U.S. government, are the focus of
the last section of the book, with articles that examine ways to respond to economic globalization on a policy level. Daisy Machado explores the impact of
globalization on the borderlands of the United States and Mexico. She challenges us to overcome negative attitudes toward those who are different, including immigrants, and to act in solidarity to uphold human dignity by promoting
policies that address global economic inequality and deplorable working conditions for those on the border and in other areas of the world. Discussion questions ask us to think about our perceptions of immigrants and immigration
history and identify how we can be in solidarity with migrants and people in
the borderlands by working to change policies.

Pamela Brubaker analyzes the neoliberal policies the U.S. government has
imposed on global economic institutions, drawing on her participation in
World Council of Churches–sponsored conversations with the World Bank and
International Monetary Fund. She argues for an "economy of life" paradigm
that calls for just, participatory, and sustainable communities and maintains
that debt cancellation, regulation of global financial speculation, and fair trade
policies will promote such a paradigm. Discussion questions raise the issue of
our responsibility for changing unjust international policies and ask readers to
envision ways to get involved on both a small and large scale.

John Cobb examines the negative environmental impacts of U.S. policies.
He argues for a Christian "bottom-up" perspective that focuses on the most vulnerable human and nonhuman creatures, as well as the planet itself. He pre-
sents already existing and imaginative alternatives to oil-dependent modes of
farming and city designs that would promote sustainability. Discussion questions ask how we can live more sustainably and what kinds of public policies
would follow from a "bottom-up" perspective.

Mary Hobgood shows how the affluent also have a stake in the struggle for
justice. She advocates an ethic of solidarity and accountability with all those
who struggle for social justice, citing a specific need for critical economic liter-

acy and an alternative Christian vision to that of the religious right. Discussion questions promote critical class awareness and uplift class oppression and poverty as crucial moral issues for Christianity.

While the topics covered by this book are certainly not exhaustive, they represent interesting and important examples of how individuals, households, and local communities can begin to get involved in the process of working toward justice in our current global economy. The resources of civil society (local churches and community groups) stand poised to make an enormous difference in the fate of economic globalization in our world. Several chapters in this book document examples of how this is already happening. We invite you to listen to the voice of God in our midst calling us to justice. We hope you will join us in the struggle.

## NOTES

1. This term was coined by Ada María Isasi-Díaz to replace the patriarchal and hierarchical notion of God's "kingdom" with the more egalitarian, familial term "kin-dom," which refers to a place where all our brothers and sisters (or "kin") are welcomed. See *Mujerista Theology* (Maryknoll, NY: Orbis, 1996), 103 fn. 8.
2. Sallie McFague, *Life Abundant: Rethinking Theology and Economy for a Planet in Peril* (Minneapolis: Fortress Press, 2001), 209–10.
3. Rebecca Todd Peters, *In Search of the Good Life: The Ethics of Globalization* (New York: Continuum, 2004); Cynthia Moe-Lobeda, *Healing a Broken World: Globalization and God* (Minneapolis: Fortress Press, 2002); Pamela K. Brubaker, *Globalization at What Price? Economic Change and Daily Life* (Cleveland: Pilgrim Press, 2001); Jerry Mander and Edward Goldsmith, eds., *The Case Against the Global Economy: And a Turn Toward the Local* (San Francisco: Sierra Club Books, 1997).
4. This model of capitalism as the "new world order" is not unrelated to the current "war on terror." This vision of capitalism as synonymous with democracy and freedom has been adopted by the Bush administration as it seeks to impose its vision of a democratic-capitalist political economy on other countries. Some charge that the Bush administration's attempts to keep the public overly fearful of terrorist attacks is a strategy to divert attention away from the economic difficulties many families face. While terrorism is certainly a serious concern, we must retain the capacity for critical ethical analysis of political and economic policies.
5. Robert E. Scott and David Ratner, "NAFTA's Cautionary Tale," Issue Brief #214, Economic Policy Institute, 20 July 2005, available online at www.epinet.org.
6. Protest erupted in this case. See http://www.citizen.org/documents/Bolivia_(PDF).PDF.
7. See Globalization and Inequality Group, The Brookings Institution, www.brookings.edu.
8. Hans-Peter Martin and Harald Schumann, *The Global Trap: Globalization and the Assault on Prosperity and Democracy,* trans. Patrick Camiller (London: Zed, 1996), 3.
9. http://www.faireconomy.org/research/CEO_Pay_charts.html (accessed July 14, 2005).

10. http://www.faireconomy.org/research/income_charts.html (accessed July 14, 2005).
11. United Nations, *Human Development Report 1999* (New York: Oxford University Press, 1999), 104–5.
12. See the Center for International Education's Online Internet Guide "Understanding the Face of Globalization" for organizations doing research on this issue: http://www.uwm.edu/Dept/CIE/Resources/globalization/globalenv.html.

# PART ONE
# HOUSEHOLD STRATEGIES

# Chapter 1

# Supporting Community Farming

*Rebecca Todd Peters*

Dogwood Springs Farm in Burkesville, Kentucky, is a ninety-acre organic farm run by the Korrow family. Eight years ago, frustrated by both corporate competition that undercut prices for their organic garlic and the difficulties associated with local marketing, the Korrows joined a growing localized, grassroots movement known as Community Supported Agriculture (CSA). Now, rather than having to transport their crops to local farmers' markets, or arrange to sell them to local independent groceries (which are themselves rapidly disappearing), for twenty-five weeks of the year the Korrows provide a bushel of seasonal, organic fruits and vegetables to a group of thirty urban families in Nashville. Each family buys a seasonal share in the farm for $600, which is paid up front. The money enables the Korrows to purchase seeds and cover their annual expenses and provides the farm with a stable consumer base. Consumers benefit by getting to know and develop relationships with the family who is growing their food and by having access to locally grown, fresh, organic products. This alternative market model challenges the dominant neoliberal economic wisdom about trade, profits, and agriculture in general. But more than serving as merely an alternative economic model, it also reveals an alternative ethical paradigm reflecting a vision of the good life that contradicts the dominant attitudes of success and happiness promoted by capitalist media outlets and the business machines that run them. CSA is one example of a larger movement within the farming community that focuses on embracing and promoting an agrarian ethic of sustainability and biodiversity. This alternative ethic challenges the corporate model of agribusiness that has come to dominate global food production in the last quarter century. Let us examine each of these approaches to agriculture and their underlying value systems in turn.

## CORPORATE AGRIBUSINESS AS A REFLECTION OF NEOLIBERAL GLOBALIZATION

While various forms of farming implements have been engineered and used throughout history in agricultural societies, John Deere introduced his first "all steel, non-sticking, unstoppable moldboard plows" to the farming community in 1837.[1] These early steel plows began the transformation of traditional farming practices, ushering in a new era of invasive farming techniques. Plows, tractors, harvesters, and other high-tech farming equipment have eased the physical burden of farmers' backbreaking work. They have also contributed to increased crop yield and efficiency in farming. Conventional American farmers embraced this new technology in the latter decades of the nineteenth century, and by the 1930s over a million tractors were working U.S. soil.[2]

The end of World War II saw a number of social and technological changes that contributed to the rise of a model of corporate-driven agriculture that has greatly transformed the production of food in our world. With the destruction of much of the European continent, the Marshall Plan's commitment to help feed and rebuild Europe after the war increased the demand on American agricultural production. Additionally, pesticides like DDT that had been used in the war to control lice and malaria were subsequently marketed to farmers as a cheap and effective way to control crop-eating insects. A barrage of chemical herbicides promised equally beneficial results in controlling weeds. Technological equipment like mechanical foggers and aerial sprayers, also developed for use in the war, were soon adapted for agricultural use and marketed to farmers. The postwar boom and prosperity enticed many farmers to live like their urban counterparts, which often resulted in one of two things: an increased need for cash to purchase consumer goods or eschewing the family farm and moving to the city in search of something new.[3] Some farmers moved to expand the size of their farmlands and try to increase profits, while others sold off land to neighbors or corporate farms and moved to the city. All of this contributed to the changing face of farming communities in the United States.

Since the 1950s farm policy and agricultural experts have greatly emphasized efficiency, which they define as increased crop yield. They argue that the best way to achieve this efficiency is through a practice known as "monocropping." Monocropping is a highly industrialized farming process that focuses on planting a single crop and often utilizes genetically enhanced "high-yield" seeds and intensive herbicides and pesticides. This type of large-scale farming also requires the use of large, fossil-fuel-driven farming equipment. As farms grow bigger and shift to more industrial models of agriculture, they often adopt the monocrop approach to agriculture in an attempt to ensure the highest yield. Theoretically this means that their land is producing at its highest potential value and the highest profits will result.

In the 1970s this industrial model of agriculture, formerly called "agribusiness," was dubbed "the Green Revolution" and was heavily promoted by development theorists who urged farmers in the two-thirds world to produce crops for export rather than for local food consumption. Agribusiness was endorsed and promoted by the World Bank and the International Monetary Fund (IMF), who cooperated with corporations and local governments to provide initially low-cost, hybridized, "high-yielding" seeds to farmers. The Bank also financed many of the large water projects that were necessary for irrigating industrial-style farms. As the structural adjustment crisis of the 1980s squeezed many poorer countries, however, new policies by the Bank and the IMF eliminated government-supported national seed banks and low-interest loans for farmers.[4] This style of farming is best suited for large, corporate style farms and for creating crops for sale on large markets. As a result, more and more farmers in the two-thirds world are growing industrial monocrops for export rather than food for local consumption.

The growing world population has also driven the development of agribusiness as conventional agronomists argue that the only way to feed the increasing world population is to increase the productivity of the land. As we have seen, the dominant perspective argues that this is best achieved through a highly industrialized form of agriculture that relies heavily on chemicals, machinery, and monocropping. All of the values promoted by this form of agriculture— increased efficiency, growth for trade, and increased economy of scale—are consistent with the values and ideals promoted by the neoliberal vision of economic development and increased global integration.

## BIODYNAMIC AND ORGANIC FARMING AS AN ALTERNATIVE AGRICULTURAL VISION

A growing and important movement in agriculture has taken various forms in recent years. It is known by different names—biodynamic, organic, or small-scale farming. In this movement, we find small-scale farmers who orient their attitudes about farming around the values of sustainability and integration. Biodynamic farming focuses on small farms that have a mutually enhancing balance of animals and plants. The plants feed the animals, as well as the humans who tend the land, and the animals, in turn, provide manure for natural fertilization of the plants, as well as dairy products and meat. Every aspect of a biodynamic farm is integrated to reduce waste, maximize efficiency and production through natural processes, and create a space in which humans, animals, and the earth can live together in mutually sustaining ways. Organic farming is also oriented toward natural pest control, fertilization, and soil enhancement, and it uses natural rather than chemical or synthetic elements to achieve these results. Both biodynamic and organic farming are better suited to small-scale farming than to large corporate farms. In recent years, though, the advent of corporate-style "organic" farms has generated division and debate within the alternative agriculture movement.

In addition to these farming movements, a new consumer movement known as the "Slow Food" movement is gaining interest and support in many places around the world. Here consumers around the world who object to the standardization of food and the increased emphasis on "fast food" have joined together to promote a slowing down of our food practices and dietary habits. What they mean to do is promote consumer attention to the origins of our food and more careful attention to its preparation—neither of which happens in a "fast food" culture. This movement was initially born in 1986 when Carlo Petrini organized a protest of the opening of a McDonald's near the Spanish Steps in Rome. He armed his protestors with bowls of homemade penne as a symbolic gesture embracing the local culture and cuisine in defiance of the values of generic, standardized fast food represented by the Golden Arches. The Slow Food movement now claims 80,000 members in 100 countries, including 140 local chapters (or *convivia*) in the United States. Proponents of slow food advocate for local farmers, promote regional food traditions, and work toward developing community appreciation and support for sustainable agriculture and the joy of growing, harvesting, and preparing food. Local education is often done through workshops, potlucks, and partnership programs with local schools to help engender appreciation in young people.

Small-scale farmers and many environmentalists are highly critical of the high-tech methods promoted by corporate agribusiness that were intended to increase efficiency and production but have had unexpected negative environmental and social side effects. Since 1960 we have lost half of the topsoil in this country, and we continue to lose it at a rate "17 times faster than nature can create it."[5] This is largely a result of the deeply invasive rupture of the soil caused by modern plowing techniques. Additionally, the overuse of chemical fertilizers, pesticides, and herbicides combined with the high-tech equipment necessary for larger-scale production has increased the capital expenses of conventional farmers compared to small-scale organic and biodynamic farming techniques that are modeled on integration and sustainability.

The push toward a corporate model of farming and increased agricultural exports is having detrimental effects on the viability of small-scale farmers. A major drive to increase U.S. grain exports in the 1970s contributed to an increase in farm size, which meant one-third fewer farmers between 1970 and 1992.[6] Peter Rosset of the Institute for Food and Development Policy notes that "while U.S. farm exports jumped from less than $10 billion to more than $60 billion per year, average farm income dropped by almost one-half."[7] The upshot is that corporate agribusinesses now manufacture and market over 95 percent of the food in the United States and have seen markedly increased profits, while small-scale family farming has almost disappeared. Furthermore, the health and quality of farmland and local waterways are rapidly deteriorating, issues that are not reflected in the economic analysis of the "success" of corporate farming.[8] The domination of the food industry by a handful of transnational corporations has contributed to the marginalization of small farmers as an integral part of the world's food supply. Instead of individual farmers and their families reaping the benefits of their labor and reinvesting their earnings in their local communities, profits are now largely shared by corporations and their investors.

Despite corporations' dominance in the market and their claims of increased crop yield, small-scale farmers have questioned the definition of efficiency used by the corporate farming community. As we have seen, corporate farmers define efficiency by focusing on crop yields, which they have been able to increase as a per-acre measurement through monocropping farming techniques. Small-scale farmers, in contrast, look more holistically at the total output of their farm rather than the productivity of crop acreage. From this vantage point, small-scale farmers argue that their farms have a higher total output per unit acre than conventional farms. In their calculations, small-scale farmers measure *all* their inputs and externalities, which might include such things as manure and compost generated on the farm for fertilizer rather than having to purchase fertilizer from an external source. Their calculations also offer a more accurate account of environmental effects like pollution and soil erosion, which corporate farmers do not include in their accounting. In addition to demonstrating a higher output for small farms than corporate farms, small-scale farmers argue that their method of calculating the "efficiency" of a farm is more accurate than crop yield per acre precisely because they do not externalize their environmental costs.

Yet another problem of industrial models of agriculture is their drive for standardization. The definition of quality in produce, for example, has been reduced to visual aesthetics. Farmers must focus on ensuring that every tomato, apple, and head of lettuce in the grocery store *looks* the same, often regardless of the taste. This standardization of crops has eliminated the natural biodiversity that farmers and nature cultivated over the centuries. While thousands of varieties of rice were once grown in the Philippines, 98 percent of the rice now comes from two varieties. Mexico has lost more than 80 percent of its maize varieties since 1930, and China has lost 90 percent of its wheat varieties in the last twenty years.[9]

It is not surprising that the perspectives of small-scale farmers and corporate agribusiness are so noticeably different, for these two groups of farmers see, understand, and experience the world differently. To large-scale farmers farming is a business enterprise and their concern is primarily economic profit. As we have seen, this profit is often bought at the cost of the health of the land and appreciation for and attention to the biodiversity of the environment. While large-scale farmers are certainly attuned to the tastes and desires of the market (as is any good businessperson), they often seem to be out of touch with what is best for the land, for our environment, and for the human community. To be fair, large-scale farmers claim to be concerned about the problem of hunger. From their perspective, the only way to feed the world is through large-scale farms and corporations managing the market. Archer Daniels Midland, one of the largest corporate agribusinesses, illustrates this view by calling itself "the supermarket to the world."

Small-scale farmers, in contrast, are more concerned that their farming practices exist in harmony with their environment and that they promote thriving local communities. They have learned that what is best for the environment is, in the long run, also best for their livelihood as farmers. Agricultural economists define "real farmers" as those who make a living from farming.[10] Many small-scale farmers live on their farms and produce food to feed themselves and sometimes others in their families and communities. They may supplement their farming with part-time or full-time work and thus do not by definition "qualify" as farmers. Farmer Gene Logsdon describes his life in the following way:

> I come closer to making my living from farming in a literal sense than "real" farmers. Carol and I raise most of our food including our meat, and some for other family members, keep a garden almost an acre in size, produce half of our home heating fuel from our own wood, derive most of our recreation and satisfaction from our farm, grow corn, oats, hay, and pasture, keep a cow and a calf, two hogs, twenty ewes and their lambs, a flock of hens and broilers, and sell a few lambs and eggs. I'm sure I spend more time *living* on our farm than any industrial farmer in our county does. When they are not golfing in Florida or fishing in Canada, they spend a lot of time in the coffee shop or in my office telling me how farming is going down the drain.[11]

Farmers like the Logsdons are often excluded from the dominant discourse about farming that drives the development of agricultural and trade policy in the United States and internationally. They simply do not have the same financial and political resources that corporate agribusiness does to shape the agricultural agenda of our world. Despite their relative lack of resources and clout, small-scale farmers are organizing around the world to promote more healthy farming practices and to support and encourage other small-scale farmers in their work.

## COMMUNITY SUPPORTED AGRICULTURE

Let us return to the Korrow family. Christy and Chris and their two daughters, Kaysha and Gabrielle, live in a round two-room home that Chris built more than a decade ago. In the midst of an overindulgent consumer culture they have chosen a radically alternative life of simplicity that carries with it both burdens and blessings. Their commitment to caring for the earth, their family, and their community is reflected in their deep sense of calling to organic farming as a spiritual expression of their deeply held values. These values reflect an "earthist" approach to the world that focuses on honoring the interdependence of our world and celebrating the sacredness of life.

Theologian John Cobb coined the term "earthist" to refer to a way of thinking and living that honors the earth and promotes sustainable human interaction with the created world. Proponents of an earthist perspective seek to reorient globalization away from individual profit-driven values toward a different set of moral norms by which supposed scientific and technological advances might be judged. The moral norms that guide the behavior of farmers like the Korrows and other earthist adherents are rooted in a respect for the sacred quality of all creation. This respect engenders sustainable methods of agriculture and behavioral lifestyles that are more in keeping with small-scale agriculture than that of corporate agribusiness.

The Korrows' recognition of this interdependence is witnessed in their own lived expression of biodynamic farming and the radical commitment they have made to living in relationship with the earth. For the Korrows, who have rejected institutionalized forms of religion, the deeply spiritual nature of their lives and their farming is evident in the way they care for their land, their crops, their animals, and one another. I first came to know the Korrows in 2000 when my family joined their CSA, Dogwood Springs Farm, which is located in rural Kentucky. During the two years that we belonged to their CSA, we visited their farm and talked with them on numerous occasions about farming, rural development, and the processes of globalization that affect our everyday lives. Like many small-scale alternative farmers, the Korrows are deeply involved in promoting sustainable agriculture and in facilitating rural and community development. The Korrows founded the Rural Center for Responsible Living in 1999, a nonprofit organization that focuses on education, outreach, and community service. They continue to work toward promoting organic and biodynamic farming in rural Kentucky and Tennessee and helping conventional farmers who are trying to switch over to more sustainable farming methods find the resources to do so.

The idea of Community Supported Agriculture first began in the United States in 1985 when farmer Robyn Van En and a core group of like-minded producers and consumers initiated the first CSA at her farm in South Egremont, Massachusetts.[12] Community Supported Agriculture is more than just a new market niche catering to urban yuppies: it is a paradigm shift away from a market-oriented and consumer-driven approach to agriculture. Organic and biodynamic farming challenge the accepted wisdom that technological advances such as chemical fertilizers and pesticides, monocropping, and all labor-saving farm machinery are beneficial achievements. CSA farmers invariably farm smaller plots of land in a much more intensive way—much like farmers did decades ago and the Amish still do today. But it is more than a different farming method that sets these farmers apart from the majority of their colleagues. Many farmers who participate in CSAs share Robyn Van En's "commitment to agriculture, to the harmony of nature and community together, to providing for 'the best hope we know of for the health and long-term thriving of our earth and its people.'"[13] Organic and biodynamic farmers embrace a different ethical vision of farming, one that is currently challenging the conventional wisdom within the farming community.

In much the same way, we as consumers must also reorient our relationship with food and the environment. American consumers are no longer used to eating with the seasons. Members of a CSA, however, receive a basket full of seasonal, local foods once a week. The lack of choice in what the week's menu will look like challenges the consumer belief that we have a right to eat whatever we want, whenever we want it, a supposed right supported by our local chain grocery store. Our absolute right to food choice and accessibility must be reassessed in light of its destructive consequences. On average U.S. food travels 1,300 miles before it lands on our table.[14] Our increased appetite for beef has contributed to the destruction of rainforests in Latin America. Land in the two-thirds world that is currently being used to grow out-of-season crops for U.S. tables could be raising food for the workers who pick it who no longer have sustainable communities and farmlands of their own. Contrary to the view of agribusiness that the only way to solve the problem of hunger in our world is to increase crop yields and production, for years we have known that the problem of food supply in our world is not one of quantity but one of distribution. Bread for the World points out:

> Virtually every country in the world has the potential of growing sufficient food on a sustainable basis. The Food and Agriculture Organization of the United Nations has set the minimum requirement for caloric intake per person per day at 2350. Worldwide, there are 2720 calories available per person per day. Over 50 countries fall below that requirement; they do not produce enough food to feed their populations, nor are they able to afford to import the necessary commodities to make up the gap. Most of these countries are in sub-Saharan Africa.[15]

Industrial agriculture and corporate distribution of the world's food supply is not the only way to address the problem of hunger in our world, nor is it the best.

But let's get back to the consumers who participate in CSAs: the basket shows up once a week and first-world consumers are challenged to eat with the seasons—to think about the weather and the land and the farmers who are growing our food. My six-year-old daughter is learning that food comes not from a grocery store, but from the land—and there are people who grow it for us. Every Saturday morning we go to the farmers' market and pick up our basket of vegetables. We talk to our current CSA farmers, Pat and Brian Bush, about what is happening on the farm, how the weather is affecting the growing season, what crops are just finishing up, and what we can expect in the next couple of weeks. In addition to visiting with the Bushes we pick up a gallon of milk from the local organic dairy, a loaf of bread from a local bakery, and often buy other local produce to supplement what we get from our CSA.

As an essentially urban child with two professional parents, my daughter's moral formation is taking place within the context of experiencing her interdependence with the land, with nature, and with other people. We have visited our CSA farms with her since she was a toddler and she is developing her own relationships with local farmers and producers in our community. As a feminist ethicist and a mother, I am deeply concerned about the moral formation of my daughter. Children do not learn simply by listening to what we say; their moral formation is shaped and formed by the actions in which we participate together as a family and as a community of people. It is not enough for me simply to explain to my daughter about social injustice and about environmental degradation. Volunteering as a family with a local homeless shelter for families opens up opportunities for us to talk about homelessness, poverty, and other social problems in ways that have meaning for a six-year-old. Likewise, visiting the farmers' market and the farms where our vegetables, eggs, and flowers come from and knowing the people who cultivate these products reinforces our own commitment to enjoying "slow food" as we cook together as a family and teach her the joys of growing, harvesting, and preparing food to share with others.

Food is essential for life, but it has more than instrumental value. Food can help us to stay in touch with God's good creation. It can serve to remind us of the bounty of the earth and the rich diversity of taste, texture, color, and smell that are available to us in different regions and areas of the world. While we must be careful not to reduce our appreciation for other cultures into simple culinary interest, food can be a window into the heart of a community and its people. Living in a culture of obesity and excess as we do in the United States, we ought to pay more attention to what and how we eat for a number of reasons. Watching our waistline is only the most self-interested of these. Attention to what we eat, where and how it is grown, and how it is prepared are central ethical questions for our moral community. Our capacity to respect the land as God's creation is directly related to our ability to experience our relationship to the environment and our interdependence as a species. Attending to our moral formation as members of local as well as global communities ought to be an intrinsic aspect of any model of globalization that we participate in creating.

Participation in a CSA can be challenging. The first year we belonged to a CSA, the farm had a bumper crop of bok choi. Before that summer I had bought bok choi only when a recipe called for it, and, yes, eight solid weeks of bok choi challenged our Western culinary repertoire and exhausted our cache of cookbooks. Yet eating with the seasons is a delightfully rewarding and spiritual experience. I have eaten broccoli rabe and Swiss chard for the first time in my life, and every summer I get two bushels of tomatoes that I put up as tomato sauce and canned tomatoes—food that feeds my family through the winter. A remarkable sense of pride and satisfaction has accompanied my participation in a CSA, feelings that were nurtured by the relationship that my daughter and I developed with the Korrows and the Bushes (and their animals) as we visited their farms and became friends. Eating with the seasons forces consumers to think about what we are eating, but it also provides a much fresher, more natural, and ultimately healthier diet than that of most Americans.

## CONCLUSIONS

Community Supported Agriculture is based on a vision of a different future for globalization. That vision holds that if we keep the earth as the center of our attention, then our social, economic, and political policies will reflect a respect for our interdependence with all of creation. Ultimately, earthist proponents call for a future rooted in smaller economies of scale that prioritize a turn toward the local. The freedom and creativity that often accompany the work of resistance have allowed for a space in which earthist thinkers have been able to generate a wide variety of public policy strategies that challenge the self-centered and greed-oriented model of capitalism that currently dominates society. The existence of CSAs illustrates one expression of what these smaller economies of scale might look like.

This earthist paradigm calls for an ardent need to shift away from a model of globalization as export-oriented trade and mass-produced products and toward a model of localization and "slow food." A return to local food production for local consumption could greatly increase poor people's access to food. Studies on subsistence agriculture have shown that it is efficient and sustainable and that it adequately provides for the food needs of its local producers.[16] Edward Goldsmith has pointed out:

> Even the World Bank, which has spearheaded the modernization of agriculture in the Third World, admitted in one of its more notorious reports that "smallholders in Africa are outstanding managers of their own resources—their land and capital, fertilizer and water" (World Bank 1981). Why then modernize agriculture and push the smallholders into the slums? The answer, as the report fully admits, is that subsistence farming is incompatible with the development of the market.[17]

Although subsistence farming might not be the best way of "developing the market," it is best for the environment, for the community, and for the earth. Joining a CSA, supporting your local farmers' market and other locally owned businesses, planting an organic garden, seeking out or creating a local slow food *conviva*—these are only a few ways that you and your household can begin to get involved in supporting your local economy and contributing to a more sustainable way of life for all God's creatures. Slow down, listen to the earth around you, and taste the difference it will make.

## QUESTIONS FOR DISCUSSION

1. Describe a typical week in your kitchen or at your dinner table. Where does your food come from? Who prepares the meals? Who eats them? What do you like most about mealtime? What do you like least? What ways can you imagine changing your weekly patterns to incorporate more locally grown produce?
2. Can you imagine yourself (or a group of people you know) joining a CSA? Why or why not? What are some of the impediments that you might face? How might you overcome these?
3. Peters describes how consumer spending and consumption patterns are issues of moral formation. How do you think about your own moral agency in relation to the food that you purchase and the food that you eat? How is the way that our food is grown, prepared, and consumed a moral issue?

## RESOURCES

### Books and Articles

Groh, Trauger, and Steven McFadden. *Farms of Tomorrow Revisited: Community Supported Farms—Farm Supported Communities*. Kimberton, PA: Biodynamic Farming and Gardening Association, 2000.

Kimbrell, Andrew, ed. *The Fatal Harvest Reader: The Tragedy of Industrial Agriculture*. Washington, DC: Island Press, 2002.

Logsdon, Gene. *Living at Nature's Pace: Farming and the American Dream*. White River Junction, VT: Chelsea Green, 2000.

Petrini, Carlo, ed., with Ben Watson and Slow Food Editore. *Slow Food: Collected Thoughts on Taste, Tradition, and the Honest Pleasures of Food*. White River Junction, VT: Chelsea Green, 2001.

Shuman, Michael H. *Going Local: Creating Self-Reliant Communities in a Global Age*. New York: Routledge, 2000.

Vitek, William, and Wes Jackson. *Rooted in the Land: Essays on Community and Place*. New Haven, CT: Yale University Press, 1996.

## Organizations and Web Sites

Alternative Farming Systems Information Center. www.nal.usda.gov/afsic.
Robyn Van En Center for CSA Resources. www.nal.usda.gov/afsic.
Sustainable Agriculture Research and Education. www.sare.org/csa.
Green People. www.greenpeople.org/csa.htm.
Slow Food USA. www.slowfoodusa.org.
Agricultural Policy Analysis Center. www.agpolicy.org.

# NOTES

1. Peter Warshall, "Tilth and Technology: The Industrial Redesign of Our Nation's Soils," in *The Fatal Harvest Reader: The Tragedy of Industrial Agriculture*, ed. Andrew Kimbrell (Washington, DC: Island Press, 2002), 169.
2. Ibid.
3. Gene Logsdon, *Living at Nature's Pace: Farming and the American Dream* (White River Junction, VT: Chelsea Green, 2000), 5.
4. Debi Barker, "Globalization and Industrial Agriculture," in *Fatal Harvest Reader*, 254.
5. Andrew Kimbrell, "Seven Deadly Myths of Industrial Agriculture," in *Fatal Harvest Reader*, 16.
6. Peter Rosset, "A New Food Movement Comes of Age in Seattle," in *Globalize This! The Battle against the World Trade Organization and Corporate Rule* (Monroe, ME: Common Press, 2000), 140.
7. Ibid.
8. Karen Lehman and Al Krebs, "Control of the World's Food Supply," in *The Case Against the Global Economy: And For a Turn Toward the Local*, ed. Jerry Mander and Edward Goldsmith (San Francisco: Sierra Club Books, 1996), 123.
9. Barker, "Globalization," 253.
10. Logsdon, *Living*, 211.
11. Ibid.
12. Stephanie Reph, *Robyn Van En Center for CSA Resources*. Fulton Center for Sustainable Living, Wilson College. http://www.csacenter.org/robynbio.html (accessed June 16, 2003).
13. Ibid.
14. Kathryn Casa, "Community Agriculture Puts Farmers' Face on Food," *National Catholic Reporter* 35, no. 28 (1999): 3–4.
15. David Beckman, *Bread for the World Institute*. http://www.bread.org/hunger basics/international.html (accessed June 16, 2003).
16. Edward Goldsmith, "The Last Word: Family, Community, Democracy," in *Case Against the Global Economy*, 509.
17. Ibid.

Chapter 2

# Relating to Household Labor Justly

*W. Anne Joh*

> *Relationship is constitutive of who we are and what we can become. Relationality, not rationality, is decisive for our humanity. . . . Relationship makes us or breaks us.*[1]

> *Let us love, not in word or speech, but in truth and action.*
> (1 John 3:18)

A few years ago, I found myself in a dilemma. In order to finish writing my dissertation, I needed to find someone to care for my child. For the first time, I was in a position to pay for child care, but I was not in a position to pay generously. I began to ask people what the going rate was for a part-time caregiver. Although I could not afford to pay the caregiver generously, I expected the caregiver to give of herself quite generously to my child. In fact, I expected nothing less from this caregiver than what I myself would lavish on my child. This particular situation raised many conflicting and challenging questions. Although I was saved from my own ambiguous role in this dilemma by forming a child-care co-op with parents of my son's friends, these questions and the attending discomforts remain with me.

Like myself, many women are entering into professions that demand great time commitments, often taking us away from our loved ones. These professional commitments also take women away from the kinds of household labor that women have traditionally performed. It is important to recognize that there have always been groups of women who work outside the home. Many of these women were single, or widows, or poor and working-class women who needed the extra income to make ends meet. In the last forty years, however, more middle- and upper-middle-class women have entered into the workforce, often into jobs that men have traditionally held (doctors, lawyers, professors, and middle- and upper-management positions). These jobs originally developed in a historical period in which there was a cultural assumption that workers (usually men) had someone at home (usually a wife) who cared for their material needs—preparing meals and caring for children and the home. The pressure of many of these jobs to work sixty-, eighty-, even hundred-hour workweeks left many professionals with little time for home, family, and leisure activities. The first generation of women to enter these professions worked extraordinarily hard to prove themselves as capable as their male colleagues. Many of them ended up working a double shift (one in the office and another at home—cooking, cleaning, and caring for children) or hiring someone else to help with the completion of household labor tasks. In the majority of cases, it is poor, working-class, or immigrant women who are hired to fulfill these responsibilities.

My generation represents a new group of professional women who are beginning to question the assumptions of the marketplace that keep such a system in place. Is it necessary for professionals to work such ridiculously long hours, particularly in an economy where we need to develop more jobs? Why is it that in the last forty years as more women have entered the workplace, men's roles and responsibilities pertaining to household labor have not shifted significantly? Why is household labor, which is essential for the success of the formal economy, so little valued and so underpaid, particularly when caring for and raising children is one of the most significant social and moral tasks in society? I have often asked how, as a middle-class Christian in a position to pay for someone else's labor, I might participate in creating alternative practices to those of the exploitative global economic order. It is vital, for everyone's sake, that we form ways of living and making a living that not only sustain us but push toward life in abundance.

This chapter is not a close examination of various economic theories, nor do I offer ultimate solutions to the economic injustices that many live under. Rather, this chapter is a theopolitical reflection on how we might navigate an economy that, because of patriarchal economic structures, has often left care work to women. The marginalization of "domestic labor" to women is rooted in a patriarchal assumption that domestic labor is not "real" labor. In fact, economic calculations of domestic labor are often not included in studies of national economies. My starting point is to assume that domestic labor, despite its relegation to the margins, is in itself a powerful aspect of our economic system that enables the formal economy to function. My contention is that as Christians wanting to engage in an ethic of love, we must practice creating just economies with people we employ in our households as a way to transform structures of economic injustice. My own reflections emerge out of my hybrid identity as a daughter of Korean American immigrants and as a feminist constructive theologian living in the United States. I have been victim and victimizer, oppressor and oppressed. I am always working to find ways to emancipate others and myself from multiple forms of interlocking "isms" (racism, sexism, classism) that work insidiously to paralyze the best of our moves toward liberation.

Women who seek employment as domestic laborers and caregivers often do so as a means to support themselves and their families. Some women are able to find these positions in their own towns and cities, but in recent years the globalization of our economy and the transnationalization of labor has increased the number of domestic laborers who immigrate in search of work. Whether they were born in the United States or abroad, many of these women share similar experiences of poverty, hard work, exploitation, and pain. When I think of the issue of household labor, the image of "living with bruised hearts" comes to mind. In this chapter I will examine the issue of household labor and what I mean by "living with bruised hearts." Just whose hearts have been bruised? In an exchange economy where everything is a commodity, how do we care if our hearts are bruised? I also introduce the norm of love through the Korean concept of *jeong* and reflect on how a metaphor of heart is vital to a collaborative emancipatory strategy of inclusivity, relationality, and economic justice making. Lastly, I will offer some strategies for practicing the norm of love/*jeong* with regard to contracted household labor.

## LIVING WITH BRUISED HEARTS: WOMEN WHO ARE PAID AS CAREGIVERS

Domestic laborers—housekeepers and child-care providers—are mostly women of color. They are the voiceless victims of imperialism, neocolonialism, globalization, sexism, racism, and classism—to name several aspects of the interconnected web of oppression that so detrimentally mars their humanity. These are also women "making a way out of no way." These are women who love fiercely, who care deeply, who sacrifice their lives on many levels in order to secure better lives for their loved ones. These are women who struggle daily with humiliation, loss of dignity and respect, verbal and physical abuse, fearful threats, and economic injustice at the hands of the people for whom they work, in the jobs that their employers would often rather not perform. These are women who, on a daily basis, incur new wounds in their hearts. However, they are also women with agency, women making difficult decisions, often choosing to leave their own children in the care of others and travel to foreign lands to participate in the global marketplace.

Rowena Bautista left her children with her mother in the Philippines to come to work as a nanny in Washington, DC, as she could not make ends meet at home. Her pay in the United States is what a small-town doctor would make in the Philippines. She calls Noa, the U.S. child she cares for, "my baby." One of Noa's first words was "Ena," short for Rowena. She gives Noa what she cannot give to her own children. In turn, Noa makes Rowena "feel like a mother."[2] Rowena's separation from her own children is a matter of concern, but she has been able to help support her family at home, as she had hoped. Other women are not so fortunate.

Many immigrant women who travel to the first world to work as domestic laborers are particularly vulnerable to employer abuse, which can be exacerbated by poor language skills and a lack of knowledge about their legal rights. A particularly shocking story is the case of Marie Jose Perez, who left Bolivia to work for a human rights lawyer in Washington, DC. Marie hoped to support her family in Bolivia with her wages as a live-in maid. However, the lawyer confiscated her passport, forced her to work twelve-hour days, and paid her less than $1.00 per hour. She could not leave the house unless accompanied by her employer. When a friend of her employer raped her, the lawyer would not take her to the hospital, giving the excuse that medical care would be too expensive.[3]

These women are part of the phenomenon that Barbara Ehrenreich and Arlie Hochschild describe as "the globalization of mothering." A "care deficit" has developed in affluent countries like the United States, as more women take demanding, high-paying jobs, which makes it more difficult for them to meet the care needs of their families. Since neither men in families nor the state (particularly the United States, which has no strong tradition of a welfare state) has stepped up to help take responsibility for meeting these needs, global care chains of nannies, maids, and sex workers have emerged. Women come from the third world and formerly communist countries to be caregivers in the first world.

The care deficit in the first world pulls migrants with the lure of unheard-of wages in their home countries, while poverty and lack of opportunity in their home countries pushes them. Like other aspects of women and globalization, such as factory work in free-trade zones, the growing market demand for domestic work is a complex reality that offers both opportunity and exploitation. While most of the women choose to immigrate in search of work that offers better economic compensation than what is available to them in their home countries, circumstances force most of these same women to leave their own children and families behind and to perform caregiving work for someone else's children and families. While there may be joy in caring for others, it can also be heartbreaking to know that while you are teaching someone else's child to talk and walk, you are not able to experience the same joys with your own children. Given the choice of staying in their home countries with work that paid a living wage or immigrating to work in the care economy of the first world, most women would stay with their homes and their families. Unfortunately, the devastating economic reality of many developing countries means that women's choices to immigrate in search of paid work are not always so "free."

The globalization of child care and housework brings the career-oriented women from affluent countries into contact with struggling women from countries that suffer in the capitalist marketplace. This contact zone is problematic and more than merely uncomfortable. It forces us to realize once again that sisterhood does not make women natural allies. In the context of globalized child care and housework, women meet each other not only across race and class divides, but across vast oceans of privilege and opportunity. This "global redivision" of women's traditional work is changing our understanding of dependency. Usually we think that poorer countries are dependent on affluent countries, for economic aid and investment, technology, or medical innovations and drugs. Now it is people in affluent countries who find themselves in need of women who are willing to provide domestic labor in roles that have traditionally been referred to as "caregiving." The preparation of food, the cleaning of one's most private areas of the home, tending to the physical (and often emotional) needs of a child or an elderly parent—all of these tasks are physically necessary for life to continue, but even more importantly these are tasks of the heart. That is why they are often referred to as caregiving tasks. An intrinsic part of the work of household labor stemming from the dependency of small children and older adults often engenders a deep emotional connection and attachment on the part of both caregivers and care receivers. In the best of circumstances this kind of relationship is one of mutual dependency and functions in mutually beneficial ways to build up our personhood. Unfortunately, when this work is not respected, honored, adequately compensated, or must be given at the expense of caregiving to one's own family (as is often the case for immigrant women), these kinds of relationships easily become exploitative.

Even if the relationship is not exploitative, inherent tensions can arise. Dominique, an immigrant from Trinidad, cares for a small child in New York. He is very close to her since she is the one who cares for him every day. Dominique observes that the parents get jealous and angry when "the kids get attached to you, because you're the one who's always there." Sally, an Irish friend of Dominique's who is also a nanny, adds: "When you leave, the children can be devastated—and it can break your heart too." These stories show us some of the ways that hearts can get bruised.[4]

We who are reading this text are more likely in a position to engage other women to do the work that we would rather not or cannot perform because of time constraints. Given the situation of need on both sides, how might we navigate such a relationship of apparent power discrepancies? How might we reconfigure our understanding of work so that it is not robbed of dignity and value? How might we reconfigure our understanding of domestic work and caregiver roles so that the economic value of the worker and the work is not denigrated? Can we dare to dream of reconfiguring our participation in contracted household labor so that it is one of justice and mutuality rather than a reification of patriarchal and imperialistic economic structures? How do we relate with one another so that even as we attempt to find just economic practices, we are mindful of how we cause "new wounds" in one another's hearts? How do we part with capitalist ways of thinking that ask how to pay as little as possible while demanding the maximum for our money? How might we disrupt and disorder this traditional, patriarchal, imperialistic global capitalism in ways that foster radical resistance at the most fundamental and intimate level of relationality? How might we recognize that especially with child-care work, our demand that our caregivers love our children is brutally unjust when we ourselves do not know how to love their children? How might we understand love "as an unfairly distributed resource"[5]—extracted from one place and enjoyed somewhere else? We are asking our caregivers to undergo heart transplants to care for our children, while their own children are left behind to suffer. What do we do when one of the costs of our children being loved is the undeniable loss and suffering paid by children in the third world? How do we exorcize our minds of capitalist constructions that see no evil in our everyday ways of squeezing the other's heart and causing "new wounds" on unsuspecting brothers and sisters? How do we form alliances that are just and cooperative? For indeed, this continuing infliction of wounds is globalization's pound of flesh.

## PRACTICING *JEONG* IN THE GLOBAL INFORMAL ECONOMY

Given the obvious economic disparity between the employer and the employee, how might we subvert an economic system that relies on injustice to maintain its power structure? How might we, in our daily living, practice an ethic of love that orients us toward a recognition of our interdependence with one another; that challenges us to find new ways of living incarnationally with one another; that is deeply committed to loving our neighbors as we love ourselves; and that is committed to loving all children as our own? Such a love would entail not only temporary and privatized solace from one another, but giving up privileges to bring justice and emancipation for all our bruised humanity. Such a love would recognize that each of us comes from a mother who labored in pain to give us life. Such a love would hear the cries of children around the world. Such a love would respond with compassion and heart, reaching out to those who are wounded and hurt by the current economic arrangements.

What form would a just relationship of reciprocity, interdependence, and mutuality look like? The kind of relationship I envision here is one that is open to acknowledging mutual receiving and giving. In this just relationship, power discrepancies are not ignored or erased, but rather examined for ways in which we might constructively counter them by forming new ways of interacting with one another and even possibly constructing new structures of economy.

One way of embracing love is to reimagine the ways in which we are in relationship with one another. I will do this through an exploration of the metaphor of heart and by reconfiguring and reimagining love with and through the Korean concept of *jeong*.

Christian theologian Rita Nakashima Brock has noted: "We know best by heart." When we live within the fullness of our heart, our lives' brokenness becomes whole and healed. Such "fullness of the heart" creates and sustains our sense of relational interconnectedness. Fundamental to Brock's understanding is the assertion that erotic power (or the power of our primal interrelatedness) is "the power of life." Relational existence is the "heart of our being, our life source, our original grace." Brock seems to suggest that erotic power comes from and enables mutual relationships. But as we have seen, rarely are globalized relationships of domestic labor mutual. The Korean concept of *jeong* can be helpful in reconfiguring and reimagining love in light of unequal relationships. This concept emerges out of relationships that are often not based on mutuality. *Jeong* emerges within the paradoxical and ambiguous space between hate and love, the oppressed and the oppressor, the self and the other, and the divine and the world.

Unfolding the Korean character for *jeong* reveals its multidimensional characteristics. Its multiple shades of meaning derive mainly from the notions of heart, compassion, and vulnerability.[6] Furthermore, when the characters that create the word for *jeong* are examined separately, we see that the core characters are "heart," but also "life" when used as a noun, and "arising, emerging out of in-betweenness" when used as a verb. The last meaning signifies a genesis of becoming that is intimately linked with connectedness and heart. It connotes an ongoing process of incarnation.

The metaphor of heart in *jeong* denotes understanding another person's plight even if one is the oppressor. *Jeong* embodies a radical sense of openness and recognition of the Self with the Other. It encompasses a profound sense of empathy similar to social theorist bell hooks's understanding of radical empathy as crossing "boundaries of class, race, [and] gender" and serving as a basis for "solidarity and coalition." Although employers may not see themselves as oppressors since they are providing work to those who want it, it is important to recognize the unequal power and status of people who employ domestic labor. Can the employer understand the pain his/her employee may be feeling—the pain of being far from home, from family? This metaphor of heart also entails recognition of the "bruised" humanity that is part of all of our brokenness and encompasses compassion and deep understanding that compels one to seek justice and forgiveness.

*Jeong* actively calls us to recognize the Self in the Other as a form of collaborative compassion. This collaboration with compassion is not one that seeks to maintain the status quo or to perpetuate oppression. Rather, such collaboration and solidarity, born out of connectedness, seeks to work toward emancipation for all. A popular saying in Korea is "you die—I die, you live—I live." This phrase, which embodies the extreme sense of *jeong* that emerges within relationality, might be uncomfortable for the Western individualistic sensibility.

Foremost, *jeong* demands vulnerability. In seeking vulnerability, we are challenged to think beyond our own experience and self-interest. *Jeong's* call for vulnerability challenges us to identify with those whom we perceive to be the "other." Dominique illustrates this when she is able to identify with the emotional vulnerability of her employer's feelings of anger and jealousy. How might her employer recognize her own vulnerability? Her own anger and jealousy? Could she then go beyond herself to encounter Dominique as a person who is also vulnerable? Who may also be angry and jealous? Could they then collaborate in compassion to enhance their relationship with each other? With the child? With Dominique's children?

Jesus illustrates this deep awareness and embrace of connectedness and heart that is part of *jeong*. Jesus spoke of the new kingdom as the *basileia* economy.[7] His characterization of this new world by relationships of reciprocity, mutuality, and interdependence corresponds with *jeong*. I want to emphasize that just as Jesus embodied *jeong* for those who came into contact with him, there were those, within his constellation, who practiced *jeong* toward him. The account of the woman in the Gospel of Luke who lovingly rubs expensive oil on Jesus' feet, despite purity laws, is a key example (Luke 7:37–50). When one's heart is turned into a heart of stone, as the hearts of the disciples who criticized this woman, it is difficult to allow *jeong* into a relationship. It is only when one's heart becomes a heart of flesh, as hers was, that *jeong* arises within connectedness across lines of race and class, power and privilege.

A crucial example of Jesus' embodiment of *jeong* in his ministry is illustrated in the way he addressed Judas in the Garden of Gethsemane. When Jesus is betrayed by one of his own disciples, rather than renouncing Judas, Jesus greets him with aching words of *jeong* as "friend" (Matt. 26:50). *Jeong* can make possible an unraveling of suffering, a new connectedness, and a process of becoming—a new genesis. The metaphor of heart in *jeong* resonates with the metaphor of the unleavened bread that rises with yeast, as a symbol of the process of the "kin-dom" of God. For the arising of *jeong* (like the small yeast) within relationality is what generates the power toward the emergence of the vision and realization of the *basileia* Jesus proclaimed.

## SOME STRATEGIES FOR THOSE WITH HEARTS OF FLESH

Our search to promote an ethic of love and create just economies in household labor must incorporate several strategies. One of the most important is to rethink our understanding of domestic labor and caregiver work. Traditional economics does not treat household labor as "real work," a perception rooted in a patriarchal understanding of such work as "private work" and thus domesticated work and not part of the real economy. One of the challenges is to make domestic labor and caregiver work visible as public work. For it is often the case that not only is the dominant economic structure unjust to these workers, but the relegation of this type of work as "private" and "informal" leaves workers vulnerable to the kind of exploitation that often has no way of being redressed. The informality thus leaves most domestic laborers and caregivers open to forms of exploitation that cannot be legally challenged. Making visible and making formal what often constitutes the informal economy challenges all women "to campaign and organize around issues of migration and domestic labor, starting first with the demand that contracted household labor be treated like jobs in the formal economy."[8]

Another strategy is to practice relational autonomy. Our appropriation of the power to recognize the Self within the Other, as well as the Other within the Self, must be balanced by maintaining distinctions of identity. This is particularly important in the employer/employee relationships of care work performed in the home. It is common for the employer to tell the employee that she is "one of the family." At first glance, this may seem like a way of establishing connection. However, one researcher found that "the disadvantages of being 'one of the family' far outweighed the advantages. Wages tended to be lower and erratically paid."[9] Certainly, employers should respect their employees, but they must not forget the unequal power dynamic that is the basis of their relationship. Thus we can recognize that care work is inherently relational and can often lead to viewing the employee as one of the family, while also respecting an employee's autonomy and dignity by being aware of the inherent power differentials of an employer/employee relationship.

Perhaps the most important strategy is to pay fair wages and offer just working conditions. If you employ domestic workers or caregivers directly, negotiate a contract that recognizes the value of the work done and the value of the person doing it. One direct way of moving toward just economic relationships is to actively support the unionization of care workers. It is important to know and follow legal standards for wages, overtime, and social security payments for household employees. These are minimum standards, however. A higher standard would be based on a living wage for your area. This information can usually be found through a local newspaper or economic justice group. In addition to pay, there ought to be clear boundaries on what the job expectations are and the number of working hours entailed. Too often, employers tack on extra jobs or hours indiscriminately. If we are to treat household labor like jobs in the formal economy, then workers should have free time apart from work; and if we are to treat workers as autonomous agents apart from our family, then workers should have the freedom to know what we expect of them and when we expect them to work.

I have suggested in this chapter that we are fundamentally relational. Inasmuch as we are relational, then we are required to explore what kinds of relationships we construct among ourselves, especially when our engagement with one another begins its basis within an exchange economy that is often not just, but exploitative. By specifically examining the metaphor of heart through the Korean concept of *jeong*, I have offered ways that we might transform the foundation of how we reimagine our relationality. I envision an informal economy that begins not with commodification of the human being and work of care, but rather with the enfleshment of the heart. This chapter is an invitation to engage in the liberatory practice of bringing heart to the work of household labor. To care means one is always involved with affection, intimacy, attention, and above all attending to one another's heart. There are many places where we encounter one another and where care for one another through domestic or child and elder care takes place. Each encounter is an opportunity to practice what we preach, that is, to love one another not only in word but in deeds.

## QUESTIONS FOR DISCUSSION

1. Who did the caregiving work in your family of origin? What about in your present family/household arrangement? Why was/is the caregiving structured this way? Are there any issues of injustice that you can identify in the distribution of caregiving tasks in your household? If so, what might you do to rectify these injustices?
2. Why is household labor so undervalued in our society? What might we do as individuals and communities to revalue and relate to household labor justly?
3. Do you (or does anyone in your family) employ someone to assist in tasks of domestic labor in your household (cooking, cleaning, child care, lawn care, etc.)? How would you describe your relationships (financial, social, emotional) with this person? How might you envision transforming these relationships in light of Joh's discussion of *jeong*?

## RESOURCES

### Books and Articles

Anderson, Bridget. *Doing the Dirty Work? The Global Politics of Domestic Labor.* London: Zed, 2000.

Applebaum, Eileen, Thomas Bailey, Peter Berg, and Arne Kalleberg. *Shared Work/Valued Care: New Norms for Organizing Market Work and Unpaid Care Work.* Economic Policy Institute, 2002. Available at http://www.epinet.org.

Chang, Grace. *Disposable Domestics: Immigrant Women Workers in the Global Economy.* Cambridge, MA: South End Press, 2000.

Ehrenreich, Barbara, and Arlie Russell Hochschild, eds. *Global Woman: Nannies, Maids, and Sex Workers in the New Economy.* New York: Metropolitan Books, 2003.

Hondagneu-Sotelo, Pierrette. *Doméstica: Immigrant Workers Cleaning and Caring in the Shadows of Affluence.* Berkeley: University of California Press, 2001.

Salazar Parrenas, Rhacel. *Servants of Globalization: Women, Migration and Domestic Work.* Palo Alto: Stanford University Press, 2001.

## Organizations and Web Sites

Break the Chain Campaign. www.ips-dc.org/campaign.

Coalition for Humane Immigrant Rights of Los Angeles. www.chirla.org.

Interfaith Worker Justice. www.nicwj.org.

International Organization for Migration. www.iom.int.

# NOTES

1. Eleazar S. Fernandez, *Reimagining the Human: Theological Anthropology of Response to Systemic Evil* (St. Louis: Chalice Press, 2004), 187–88.
2. Arlie Hochschild, "Love and Gold," in *Global Woman: Nannies, Maids, and Sex Workers in the New Economy,* ed. Barbara Ehrenreich and Arlie Hochschild (New York: Metropolitan Books, 2003), 16.
3. Joy M. Zarembka, "America's Dirty Work: Migrant Maids and Modern-Day Slavery," in *Global Woman,* 142–43.
4. Susan Cheever, "The Nanny Dilemma," in *Global Woman,* 35.
5. Hoschchild, "Love and Gold," 22.
6. There are multiple contours to the concept of *jeong* in Korean. According to the *Minjung Essence Korean-English Dictionary* (Seoul: Hollym International Corporation, 1996) there are three derivatives of *jeong* : (1) *ae-jeong*, which comes very close to the word "affection," which emerges out of relationship with one's spouse/partner, between parent and child, and between people in intimate relationship (not necessarily sexual); (2) *ihn-jeong*, which means compassion, sympathy or, as I maintain, a recognition of one's humanity in the face of the Other; and (3) *gahm-jeong*, which means feelings or intuition within a relationship.
7. *Basileia* is the Greek term for "kingdom."
8. Bridget Anderson, "Just Another Job? The Commodification of Domestic Labor," in *Global Woman,* 114.
9. Ibid., 112.

# Chapter 3

# Consuming Responsibly

*Marcia Allen Owens*

In the United States, consumer debt and personal bankruptcies have reached record highs. Savings rates have reached a twenty-five-year record low. We now have more cars than registered drivers. Goods that were either nonexistent or considered luxuries in the 1970s are now considered among the long list of American necessities. Houses have become landfills, repositories of the excess stuff that Americans have continued to accumulate. When our houses reach capacity, we put things in storage. The Economic Census conducted by the U.S. Census Bureau reports that in 2002, the United States' self-storage industry, an industry that was virtually nonexistent in the 1960s, earned more than $3.5 billion in revenue. There is well over 1 billion square feet of storage space available in the United States. Yet we are still in pursuit of more space. *USA Today* declared the decade that began with the year 2000 as the "decade of the exurbs," meaning that people are willing to move to and commute from the farthest edges of metropolitan areas in order to achieve the American Dream of owning a detached house with a big yard.

Many believe that globalization is synonymous with Americanization, that is, globalization is the dominance of American culture and consumer habits throughout the world. Although many countries have been able to preserve their unique cultures, the pervasiveness of this notion has led to American consumption serving as a model for the world. In this chapter I will look at the problem of individual overconsumption, emphasizing the church as a model and source of justification for our levels of purchasing and consumption. Just as American overconsumption serves as a negative model for the world, church overconsumption negatively influences individual parishioners. Individuals need to come to an awareness of the negative impacts of consumption on people and the environment and then translate this new consciousness into action by purchasing and consuming more responsibly.

## AFFLUENZA AND THE CHURCH'S ROLE

In 1997 the Public Broadcasting System aired a program called *Affluenza*, which was later developed into a book of the same name. The term "affluenza" describes the American desire to have more as a viral infection that is spreading throughout the world: "a painful, contagious, socially transmitted condition of overload, debt, anxiety, and waste resulting from the dogged pursuit of more."[1] In other words, affluenza is a dysfunctional relationship with money or the pursuit of it.

Affluenza is a socially sanctioned virus, in that it has become acceptable to engage in the excessive pursuit of things as part of achieving the American Dream. The American Dream has been continually upscaling, however. The Roper Center at the University of Connecticut has been conducting American public opinion surveys on various issues since the 1930s. One survey asks about the annual household income that would allow people to fulfill all of their dreams. In the ten years between 1987 and 1996, that income requirement more than doubled, going from $50,000 to $102,000. In a related survey, Americans were asked about the "good life" and what they would need to reach it. Responses have increasingly focused on material things and luxuries rather than happy marriages and families or interesting and socially beneficial jobs. Another survey asks: "What is the biggest problem facing you and your family these days?" Since the 1960s more than 50 percent of families surveyed responded with an answer that involves money. Most of those concerned about money say that they are concerned about not having enough money to make ends meet. While this is a legitimate reality for many Americans, we also have elevated understandings of what the basic necessities in life are.

Affluenza has been rapidly spreading over the last fifty years and increasingly claims its followers during childhood with advertising strategically targeted at youth. Ironically, Christmas has become the poster child for affluenza. The celebration of the birth of Jesus, the one who through his teachings continually warned about the problems of wealth, has now become so commercialized that

Christmas decorations are appearing in malls in October, right after Halloween. Christmas excess has spread worldwide through advertisement, to Christian and non-Christian cultures alike.

One would think that, based on Jesus' ministry, churches would offer a countercultural critique of excess consumption, but increasingly churches have succumbed to affluenza and shape their constituents accordingly. Churches readily succumb to the desire to be "bigger and better." There seems to be fierce competition to build bigger and better edifices "for God" with more space, more ministries, more services, and more comfort for "God's people." *Forbes Magazine* reports that in 1970, only ten churches fit the definition of a megachurch (non-Catholic churches with at least 2,000 members). In 1990 there were 250. In 2003 there were 740. Many of these churches achieve their growth goals by adopting corporate models, including chief executive officers, marketing plans, and the efficient and effective use of technology. One Atlanta megachurch, promoting its message of Christian prosperity, boasts that it has built a sanctuary that holds 10,000, a choir stand that holds 1,000, and a family life center, and it has cleared only 300 of the more than 700 acres with which God has blessed it.

Most churches do not consider the social and ecological impact of this "steeple envy," nor do they consider what theological and ethical message they are promoting with their model of "bigger is better." Christian ethicist Larry Rasmussen writes: "Churches *are*, not only *have*, a social ethic. They form—or malform—those whose lives are shaped by worship, instruction, moral witness, church order, or any other expression of church life. . . . [Churches] comprise a way of being in the world. Moral formation (and malformation) is the inevitable outcome of what is done (and not done) and the way in which it takes place (or fails to take place)."[2]

On one hand, neither the church nor individuals should underestimate the influence of church involvement and religious teaching and modeling on individual behaviors such as consumption and purchasing. On the other hand, churches are made up of individuals who bring their own beliefs and practices to the leadership and decision-making positions that they hold in churches. If the church membership is or aspires to be upper-middle class, then clearly the church buildings must reflect upper-middle-class standards of living. In other words, if the pastor and the church leadership live or aspire to live in McMansions, then church leadership perpetuates the belief that the church's physical structures must be the Christian McMansion "supersized."

Scripture and Christian theology can and have been used to justify overconsumption. Traditional interpretations of the Genesis creation stories provide a foundation for a dominating relationship between humanity and the rest of creation. The first creation story, beginning at Genesis 1:26, says: "Let us make humankind in our image, according to our likeness; and let them have dominion. . . . Be fruitful, multiply, and fill the earth and subdue it; and have dominion over the fish of the sea." Some people take the words "dominion" and "sub-due" quite literally, believing that humans have a God-given right to harness, dominate, and subdue all of creation for human needs and wants. The second creation story in Genesis 2 says that God placed humans in the garden to "till it and keep it." Although this passage denotes stewardship, the prevailing inter-pretation is of ownership, use, and exploitation. Unfortunately, many Chris-tians interpret these Scriptures to mean that the earth was made for humans and humans alone.

A further interpretation of the first Genesis creation story that some Chris-tians use to justify destructive behavior is God's instruction to "be fruitful and multiply." Again, many Christians have taken this instruction quite literally. It took the human population over 250,000 years to reach the one billion mark. Now, in one lifetime (fewer than 100 years), the human population is estimated to grow by another five billion. "Be fruitful and multiply" has been used to pro-mote the idea that everyone should prosper and become parents. Overpopula-tion is a problem in and of itself for environmental sustainability. The situation becomes even more acute, however, if all the billions of people in the world con-sume as much as the average American. One study claims that if the eleven bil-lion people (population estimate after 2050) had energy consumption similar to the average American, oil resources would be exhausted in 35 to 75 years.[3] Similar estimates could be made for other finite resources.

## RESPONSIBLE CONSUMPTION

Churches are responsible for setting norms through organizational rules, pro-nouncements, or denominational teachings, but churches can also informally or implicitly set norms by modeling certain behaviors, which, in turn, affect individuals' awareness, sensitivities, and behaviors. Norms can be thought of in terms of standards, customs, or rules of a particular group. Christian norms can emerge from various sources—Scripture, church tradition, theology, and expe-rience, to name a few. There is a continuity of church traditions regarding issues such as violence, poverty, and nature. Although these traditions vary based on the church form or denomination, Scripture and theology in the Christian tra-dition can guide us to alternative ways of thinking and being in the world that do not wreak havoc on other people and the environment.

While we have seen some of the ways in which Genesis has been interpreted to justify human behavior and overconsumption, other traditions of interpre-tation within Christianity lead to a more earth-centered and sustainable human community. For example, Rasmussen holds that while humans may occupy a special place of power and responsibility within creation, we ought to stand in awe of it, respecting and learning from it, as we are part of a moral and natural order that surpasses us. He interprets the divine commands "be fruitful and multiply" and "till and keep" as implying that divine creation is living, dynamic, and continuing, rather than complete and perfect. Furthermore, the same divine power who created life "beckons creation's redeeming transformation in the steady direction of compassion and justice." Thus, while life is a gift, we have a responsibility for both allowing and promoting the flourishing of creation. Such responsibility requires sustainable levels of consumption and reproduction.[4]

Genesis is not the only place where Scripture offers insight into our present ecological crisis. Overconsumption was also an issue in biblical times. In Exodus 16, when God provided enough manna to sustain the community each day, Moses instructed the people to gather as much as they needed. Those who attempted to hoard found that the manna had spoiled by the following morning. God provides for our needs, but not to excess. This passage points to the norm of sustainability, which requires that we relate to nature in a way that respects its integrity and allows all life to flourish in the long-term future. Sustainability is the practice of good stewardship by humans, with concern for the entire planet and future generations of life.

Closely related to the norm of sustainability is the norm of sufficiency, which emphasizes a basic equality in that all forms of life are to share in the resources of God's creation. Respect for all to have enough entails limits on excess, as illustrated by the famous saying, "Live simply so others may simply live." Sufficiency and sustainability are reinforcing norms. Sufficiency is more than bare survival, but if our relationship with nature is to be sustainable many of us must live more simply. Thus the norm of sufficiency is aimed specifically at those of us who have bought into the frenzy of affluenza.

One way to begin the process of raising awareness is to consider the adage, "Think globally, act locally." Thinking globally is often the biggest stumbling block. The problems of globalization are so large and overwhelming that they frequently immobilize us. Yet we regularly demonstrate that hope is still present. While hope allows us to be deeply moved by efforts to help one endangered beached whale return to the deep, we often ignore the loss of tens of thousands of other species each year simply because that problem is too large for us to deal with. It does not occur to us that humans might be the next species to be lost, that we will not necessarily be the last ones standing. We must somehow grasp the notion of thinking globally. We must confront, critique, and erase the tapes that play in our heads of how things are, how things came to be, and how they will be. We have become so accustomed to the status quo and our subconscious beliefs have become engrained so deeply in our psyches that we continue to behave in the same ways even when there is evidence of a crisis.

We are altering the entire global system with our consumption. Our insatiable desire for "bigger, better, faster" is not only filling our landfills with yesterday's toys (and the packaging it was wrapped in!) but our fossil-fuel emissions are contributing to the destruction of the ozone layer. That remarkable skin that surrounds our planet, protecting us from the sun's dangerous rays and enabling life on our planet, may very well be destroyed by human overconsumption. Our quest for prosperity and success by today's materialistic definition could render us victims of that same success through depletion of the earth's resources.

We tend to think we are entitled to material possessions, especially if we worked hard for our money. Even if we do not have the money, our sense of entitlement leads us to charge the things we cannot afford. In essence, we turn desires for status and convenience into rights. With our culture's emphasis on personal rights and freedoms, many people do not recognize how dependent we are on the well-being of the ecosystem. Before we can enjoy our individual rights and personal freedoms, we need air and water that are free of contamination. We take breathing for granted, but we need trees and other green plants to produce the oxygen we need to breathe, and they need the carbon dioxide that we and other mammals exhale in order for them to breathe. We ignore our interdependence at our own peril. Neither individuals nor societies can function well without a healthy ecosystem.

We cannot change if we are unaware of our need to change. We must achieve a new awareness, one that inverts our current ordering of priorities. Respect and care of the ecosystem must be first, followed by social and personal freedoms. In order to change our patterns of consumption we must first become aware of how our worldview has been formed and how our perspective shapes the way we see the world around us. Change is difficult, but not impossible. Eastern European countries withdrew from the communist system. Apartheid ended in South Africa. The United States changed its mind-set about smoking in a few decades. Change can happen, but it is often a long process that occurs one mind at a time. In order for our actions to change, we must change our worldview.

## EXAMINING OURSELVES

The book *Affluenza* includes some helpful questions to stimulate our awareness of what we consume, how we dispose of waste, and what our priorities in life are. Self-awareness of our actions and their effects is key to transforming our worldview and eventually our behavior. These questions about purchasing, consumption, and waste are important for both individual and church awareness. They prompt us to take stock of our consumer habits, the first step to changing our behavior. The second step is to choose one area in our life and explore where our products come from, alternative products we can buy (or even better, ways we can do with less), and how we are disposing of these products. Gradually we can critically assess more areas of our life and, one hopes, bring this awareness to the church.

First, examine where products come from, who produced them, and how they are packaged. Who made this product? Was it a union worker? Or was it made with illegal child labor? Where was this product made? Was it made in a factory with safeguards in place for the workers and the environment, or was it made in an oppressive sweatshop? Have I looked at how the products that I buy are packaged? Is there extra cardboard or plastic or outside covering? Is the packaging biodegradable?

Second, examine your purchasing behaviors. Why am I buying this? Do I need it or do I want it? Do I buy items just for convenience? Do I think that things can make me happy? Can I really afford it? Am I in debt from buying things? What systems are affected by this purchase? Is what I am buying consistent with what really matters to me? Does my church practice responsible purchasing? How much paper do we use? Do we really need a printed bulletin every Sunday? Do we have to use paper and disposable plates and eating utensils for our social gatherings? How many coffee cups do we send to the landfill each week?

Third, examine where products are disposed and the effects of this disposal. Where does this product go when I throw it away or trade it in for the newer model? Does it go to a landfill? Does it have hazardous components that contribute to environmental degradation as it decomposes? Does it leak and end up contaminating the water? Is it incinerated? Does burning it release harmful components into the air? Is it recyclable? Can it be turned into something else useful, or can it be donated and used again by someone else?

Fourth, examine the food you eat. Is the food I eat organic? Was it sprayed with pesticides that may affect my health? Did those pesticides affect the health of workers or people who lived near where the food was produced? Do I have to have bottled water, or can I use filters that create less waste? Or can I just drink tap water?

Fifth, examine the transportation you use. How many cars are there in my household? Are they fuel efficient? Do I drive alone, or do I carpool? Is public transportation available for some of my travel? Can I ride my bike or walk where I need to go? What are the environmental impacts of my chosen mode of transportation? Did I consider alternative fuel or hybrid vehicles?

Sixth, examine the environmental impact of structures and the use of energy within them. Is my home or church earth friendly? What makes a building earth friendly? Did I buy more house than I really need? Do we effectively utilize all of the space in our church? What systems were affected by its construction? Does it use energy efficiently? Do I use energy efficiently?

In addition to changes in our personal and household behavior patterns, we can also strategize about ways our churches can get involved in becoming more environmentally and socially responsible in their behaviors and practices. The last set of suggestions begins to open up this avenue of thought. As you start to think about your own congregation, one way to change the consciousness and behavior of the church is to educate the youth and have them instigate various environmental practices in the church (recycling, reusable mugs for coffee hour, community garden, etc.). These types of projects provide great opportunities for youths to work together on a project that will benefit the whole church as well as offering ample opportunity for theological reflection on creation, responsible stewardship, and consumer habits. Additionally, the enthusiasm generated by young people can be catching and can turn a church into an environmentally sustainable role model for individual members.

Another strategy is illustrated by the Community Resources for Responsible Living web site (sanjoseuu.org/ResponsibleLiving/clothing.htm) created by the First Unitarian Church of San José for their church members to share information on no-sweat clothes or shoes (i.e., not made in a sweatshop), community supported agriculture and farmers' markets, fair trade crafts, responsible tourism, and more. One of the most difficult aspects of responsible consumption is knowing where to go in your community for a variety of consumer goods and services that are both environmentally sustainable and economically just. Every community can use this kind of clearinghouse, and churches can serve as leaders in their communities in researching, supporting, and publicizing morally responsible and ethically engaged consumer habits and practices. This can be a service not only to your own congregation, but to the entire community at large.

## CONCLUSION

The impacts of globalization are widespread. Some are obvious, others are more subtle. Looking at responsible purchasing and consumption through the lens of the church reveals the interconnectedness of our individual and societal worldviews, mind-sets, and practices. Bringing about awareness through engaging in self- and community assessments regarding purchasing will increase awareness and likely lead to positive transformation—one mind at a time. Through awareness, individuals can become more responsible citizens in the global community. In turn, aware individuals may help to shape churches and faith communities to become more responsible institutional citizens in the face of globalization and the contagion of affluenza.

## QUESTIONS FOR DISCUSSION

1. For one week, keep a journal of everything that you buy (food, gas, clothing, toys, entertainment, etc.). What do you notice about your spending habits? Are there purchases that you could do without? How much waste accompanying your purchases (i.e., packaging) ended up in the trash? Discuss with your family and friends how you felt about your own consumer behavior after tracking it for a week.

2. Check the Web site for www.responsibleshopper.org to examine companies that you frequent. Were you aware of their labor and environmental practices? Will this affect whether you purchase goods from them in the future? Why or why not?

3. How can we and others become aware of our disease of affluenza? Can you identify some of the symptoms of this infection? How do we move from awareness of affluenza to changing our consumption patterns? Try to identify one area in your life where you can begin to make changes and work on that. How might you influence your community or your congregation with your new awareness and alternative behavior of responsible consumption?

## RESOURCES

### Books and Articles

Center for a New American Dream. *Responsible Purchasing for Faith Communities.* Takoma Park, MD: New American Dream, 2002.

Dawn, Marva J. *Unfettered Hope: A Call to Faithful Living in an Affluent Society.* Louisville, KY: Westminster John Knox Press, 2003.

DeGraaf, John, David Wann, and Thomas H. Naylor. *Affluenza: The All-Consuming Epidemic.* San Francisco: Berrett-Koehler, 2001.

Dunham, Laura. *Graceful Living: Your Faith, Values, and Money in Changing Times.* Indianapolis: Ecumenical Stewardship Center, 2001.

Klainer, Pamela York. *How Much Is Enough? Harness the Power of Your Money Story and Change Your Life.* New York: Basic Books, 2002.

Schor, Juliet B., and Douglas B. Holt. *The Consumer Society Reader.* New York: New Press, 2000.

### Organizations and Web Sites

Public Broadcasting System. www.pbs.org/kcts/affluenza.

New American Dream. www.newdream.org.

Responsible Shopper. www.responsibleshopper.org.

Oxfam. www.oxfam.org.uk/what_we_do/fairtrade.

No Sweat. www.nosweatapparel.com.

Alternatives for Simple Living. www.SimpleLiving.org/index.shtml.

### Videos and DVDs

*Affluenza: The All-Consuming Epidemic.* KCTS Television. 1997.

*Escape from Affluenza.* KCTS Television. 1998.

Sut Jhally. *Advertising and the End of the World.* Media Education Foundation. 1997.

*The Overspent American: Why We Want What We Don't Need.* Media Education Foundation. 2004.

# NOTES

1. John DeGraaf, David Wann, and Thomas H. Naylor, *Affluenza: The All-Consuming Epidemic* (San Francisco: Berrett-Koehler, 2001), 2.
2. Larry Rasmussen, "Introduction: Eco-Justice: Church and Community Together," in *Earth Habitat: Eco-Injustice and the Church's Response*, ed. Dieter Hessel and Larry Rasmussen (Minneapolis: Fortress Press, 2001), 18.
3. F. E. Trainer, *Developed to Death: Rethinking World Development* (London: Green Print, 1989), 61.
4. Larry L. Rasmussen, *Earth Community, Earth Ethics* (Maryknoll, NY: Orbis, 1996), 249–62.

# Chapter 4

# Eating Intentionally

*Shannon Jung*

If there is truth to the saying that we are what we eat, then the statistics on the rates of obesity and poor health indicate that we must be eating wrong. Two out of every three U.S. adults are overweight; one of those two is obese. Fifteen percent of children aged 6–19 are overweight. We may be the fattest people on earth. Not surprisingly, our rates of heart disease and diabetes are on the rise. Meanwhile, psychologists tell us that we have the highest rate of depression on the globe. (Other affluent countries have similar, if less dramatic, numbers.)

At the same time we are quite aware that many people in the world are hungry. There are 800 million people worldwide who are seriously malnourished, some 35 million of them in the United States. We are also aware that we in the United States (and other affluent nations) benefit from a global food supply system that disadvantages others, many of whom make up the 800 million malnourished people just mentioned. This produces, if not a sense of guilt, at least a sense of complicity.[1]

The problem is that the global food supply system is designed to encourage overeating by the affluent, and the delivery of that food from those peoples who are "less strategically placed." It does this in ways that poison our land, air, and water; foster unhealthy lifestyles for the affluent; threaten the lives of global peoples; and can even undermine political regimes.

In this chapter I focus on the eating practices of the affluent. I ask: What consequences does the current system of economic globalization have on the quality, safety, and availability of food? How does the global food supply system shape household spending and eating? Once we have identified some of the issues surrounding our household eating and buying habits, I commend eating practices that are healthy for ourselves, the planet, and other peoples. Finally we will attend to the issue of how these strategies might shape a new global economic system.

## GLOBAL FOODS, HOUSEHOLD IMPACT

We no longer know where our food comes from in the United States. In few sectors has the reality of globalization become more integrated into our daily lives. What enters our stomachs may have come from Guatemala or Argentina or Thailand or Tennessee. Brian Halweil claims that food travels on average 2,000 miles from its place of growth to our tables. In the United States, this represents a 25 percent increase since 1980; in the United Kingdom it is a 50 percent increase.[2]

The lengthy distance our food travels has economic and health implications. Generally speaking, the higher up we eat the processing chain—that is, the greater the distance between production and consumption—the less healthy it is. Many of the extra steps between farmer and consumer remove nutrients and fiber, and add salt, sugar, fat, and other fillers. In many cases this removes taste as well. Eating lower on the chain means that we buy more fresh fruits, vegetables, and meats that have been raised in a healthier manner.

Moreover, the farther food travels, the less money that is retained by the farmer and the rural community. Hauling, packaging, processing, and brokering eat up more of the final price and raise the price consumers pay. In addition, these increased costs end up subsidizing a system that is heavily dependent on fossil fuel.

The global system of food supply is marked by the concentration of a small number of industry giants. These corporations (e.g., Cargill, ADM, Smithfield, ConAgra, Novartis) control a large part of the production and distribution of food. In the United States the top five food retailers held 24 percent of the market in 1997; in three years that percentage had risen to 42 percent. The four largest beef firms process 81 percent of cattle; the four largest pork firms process 59 percent of pork; four chicken firms process 50 percent of all broilers. Comparable percentages of concentration for wheat and soybeans are 61 percent and 80 percent.[3] The consolidation of grocery stores further reflects the concentration of producers. Wal-Mart, for example, has skyrocketed into the lead as the nation's largest grocer, far outdistancing Kroger, Safeway, and other chains. Interesting in this respect is Wal-Mart's movement into international markets as well.

One might believe that with this concentration of production and distribution comes additional safety for the consumer. The containment response to mad cow disease discovered in the United States and foot-and-mouth disease in Great Britain would suggest that there exist food firewalls between countries. This is illusory, however. Given the degree of integration in the global system, it is hard to know exactly what one is eating or where it came from.[4] The monetary value of the international food trade has tripled since 1960 and its volume has quadrupled. The United States is the world's largest exporter of agricultural goods in the world. Three companies account for 81 percent of corn exports, and 65 percent of soybeans. The sheer volume of imports—even beef—into our country at the same time suggests a world system where microbes roam free. Efforts to adopt a "Country of Origin" label and to otherwise label sources of our food have been stymied, but there is no reason to suspect that it is only "foreign" bugs that bring disease into our country and households.

Our food supply is increasingly unsafe and unhealthy. Concentrating large numbers of animals in feedlots is a prescription for infectious influenza viruses. The growth hormones and antibiotics that are regularly used to pump up livestock productivity are leeching into our food supply, our soil, and our environment with alarming frequency. Chemical emissions of ammonia, hydrogen sulfide, and other harmful gases are producing health hazards. Pesticides and genetically modified organisms (GMOs) affect our grains and pass unknown residues into the food supply. From an environmental perspective, our present practices of production are unsustainable.

What most captures our attention, however, is what is happening to our bodies. They are, in many ways, a reflection of the national and global culture. The order and disorder of the society becomes embodied as we accept, resist, or modify the values connected to our food system. For example, positively, we celebrate the diversity of our national cuisines; most of us are probably open to eating more adventurously than we used to. Negatively, as the physical education programs in our public schools have had their funding reduced or eliminated, increasing numbers of our young people have become overweight.

The health consequences of overeating are evident. Obesity is a public health epidemic. Greg Critser notes the increase in type 2 diabetes in children, much of which can be traced to the increase in obesity caused by our high-fat diet.[5] Respiratory diseases, orthopedic problems, and allergic asthma accompany obesity. Stroke and heart attacks are on the rise. Obesity is second only to tobacco as a cause of death. Yet even as social dynamics have conspired to encourage men and women, girls and boys, to eat more and exercise less, other dynamics have sent the message that becoming overweight ("controlling our weight") is our individual responsibility. The serious eating disorders anorexia and bulimia are especially rooted in the dynamics of being a girl or woman in our nation.

Underlying many of these dynamics are corporate and government policies that support cheap food and are integrally tied to the present state of economic globalization. Such corporate policy is driven by reducing production costs and increasing profit margins. In the resulting "race to the bottom," food is produced and processed wherever it is cheapest to do so.

The deleterious effects of corporate and government policies on the environment, on rates of world hunger, on the wages of domestic and international farm workers, on rural communities, and on the healthiness and safety of our food are evident. As Wendell Berry has written, "The global economy does not exist to help the communities and localities of the globe. It exists to siphon the wealth of those communities and places into a few bank accounts. To this economy, democracy and the values of the religious traditions mean absolutely zero."[6] Can we have a different, a new, global economy? I will turn to that question in the concluding section.

All these factors affect our local households, of course. We are not impervious to the injustices that arrive on our dinner tables. Our children inherit our eating practices along with the blind eyes that we often turn as families (sometimes with regretful resignation) to the social dimension of what we eat.

## A CHRISTIAN MORAL FRAMEWORK

The Christian tradition has a rich repertoire of eating practices and guides to just, good eating. However, these very practices are themselves often shaped "by the cultural forces of global capitalism."[7] Thus it is vital that we consider both the cultural forces that shape the way that we currently eat (as we have been doing) and ask whether they embody a Christian vision of life abundant. In this chapter I have been considering three areas of particular interest to households—cost, bodies, and quality of eating practices. Elements of the Christian vision that correspond to these are that the costs of food production and eating be justly distributed; that the creation be cared for sustainably; that we honor our bodies; and that we delight in the goodness and relationships that make up our lives.

The food supply system as it presently exists in the United States contravenes these Christian values. There are some positive aspects to the system: It provides many delights and is an incredible bargain, costing us only 10 percent of our disposable income in the United States according to the U.S. Department of Agriculture.[8] Those "advantages" (for us) come at a high price, as we are seeing. Those costs are also household costs. Let us turn then to an assessment of the three areas I have identified: the cost of food, care of our bodies, and the quality of our eating practices.

## Cost

The bottom-line value for most households, regarding food, is monetary cost. The very word "value" as used in popular media has come to mean "low price." Cheap-food policies have succeeded beyond our most outrageous imagining. What is alarming is that low costs have crowded out other values as the determinant of our choices. They have disguised or hidden from us what food is and as a consequence we do not attend to food. We do not appreciate what food is, or what it really costs (not just financially) when monetary price is everything. We do not appreciate how we can meet God in our eating. As a result we are less able to teach our children a deeper, more spiritual understanding of food.

This also means that we are too often oblivious to the environmental costs of raising food. The majority of our food comes from large operations that are on the whole less oriented to the long-term sustainability of the land than small farms. Environmentally destructive agricultural practices cost far more than they save in the long term.

Another high cost comes from the resulting inability of rural agriculture to sustain adequate community services in the United States. The rates of poverty and negative social indicators in some rural areas in America exceed those of inner-city slums. Rural communities and farmers overseas are similarly hard hit. When NAFTA permits the dumping of grain cheaply on Mexican markets, those who benefit are not U.S. farmers or Mexican farmers. Crop prices and consequently farmers' profits (and sometimes their very livelihood) are undercut by these practices. It is the processors and sellers of the grain, again the industry giants, who reap the economic benefits.

## Honoring Our Bodies

Our ignorance about food causes us to dishonor our bodies. We ignore central biblical admonitions to treat our bodies as temples. Obesity was probably not a major problem in first-century Palestine; thus it is surprising that there is as much attention paid to bodily life in the New Testament as there is. Today, however, we have distanced our physical and material (and even economic) well-being from our spiritual and mental and social well-being. We believe that we can manage our eating from a control center. This is a debilitating myth with deep roots in a fragmented rather than a holistic view of ourselves. We may see ourselves as technological products awaiting a pill that will control our weight the same way we control all manner of other disorders. We are out of touch with our bodies; we eat badly; and we buy foolishly and cheaply. This insensitivity to our bodies may be one reason why dieting often fails.

## Quality of Eating Practices

Christian tradition points to numerous eating practices that relate us to God and to others: saying grace; fasting; feasting; honoring our bodies; self-examination, confession, and transformation; Eucharist; and hospitality. Just as we often neglect to care for our bodies, our households often exhibit a similarly low quality of attention to the practices, relationships, and habits that accompany eating. We undervalue ourselves and miss the delights of eating, of one another, and of relating to God. Food and eating are intended by God for our delight and our sharing. The way we currently eat cheats us of enjoyment.

Cheap food, quickly prepared, thoughtlessly eaten; eating in front of the television; and solitary eating—how can these not affect our lives? Is this life abundant? Cheap food leads to unappreciative eating, obesity and poor health, attenuated relationships, and the transmission of misperceptions to our children. Rather than contributing to our delight and the enjoyment of our households, these dynamics have reduced the joy and quality of our lives.

## EATING WELL

It is possible to reverse these practices. There are ways to eat well and enjoy our lives more. Let us consider what sorts of *household* activities—simple steps—might begin to reverse those trends that make for bad eating. We begin with cost, recognizing that nutritionally harmful food is no bargain.

### Cost

First, eat more nutritionally. Fight the impulse to equate low price with a bargain. Develop family rituals around food preparation and gathering. The benefits of shopping and cooking together are priceless, fostering camaraderie and friendship. And the food is liable to be tastier if the work is done together and one has invested herself in its preparation. How can you cost that out?

Second, recognize the hidden costs of subsidizing corporate farming. Large agricultural subsidies are not targeted toward those who need subsidies but toward large producers. (Seven percent of U.S. farmers produce 80 percent of the food on one-third of the land under cultivation. Subsidies are tied to that 80 percent.) Develop those assets—skills, low-cost markets, relationships, farms—that are local and that do not represent drains on local resources. When locally produced food replaces imported food, the household buyer saves money. The initial inconvenience could be replaced by more tasty and healthy meals, to say little of the joy of gathering the food. Furthermore, when industries are local, many of the collateral assets (jobs, sales, small businesses, and industries) stay in the community. Do a community economic assessment to determine the impact of buying in your local community in terms of how it affects sales tax revenue. See your children and neighbors as assets.

Third, shop farmers' markets. The savings that farmers realize by being able to sell their own produce represents not only lower costs to you, and a higher return for them, but also better food. It is a win-win-win situation. Also the local market is a social environment, a place to see and talk to your neighbors.

Fourth, buy local foods. Join a cooperative or exchange where a whole range of foods are offered. Dairy, vegetables, fruits, and meats are easily available as well as dry goods. Know what you are eating, how it was raised and grown, what is in season, how others cook local foods. Patronize restaurants that buy locally. Investigate where your schools or other institutions buy food and encourage them to buy locally.

Fifth, join a parish-based community development project. One such project is the Work of Our Hands initiative, begun in churches. Parishioners publicize the products and services they have to offer to one another. Many are interested in purchasing while others may want to swap services. Directories are printed and distributed; neighbors patronize, support, and promote one another. Seasonal reminders of product availability are publicized; others exhibit at local community celebrations. Besides the ability to buy quality at lower prices, buying locally is a foundation of community organization.[9]

Sixth, grow your own food. This is one of those cost-saving areas where the value realized is worth far more than money. Not only do you get educated, but you also feel pride in your work. The food tastes better and working together with family or friends or church comrades makes it taste even better! You might also gain a lively appreciation for the creation.

Seventh, get involved with Community Supported Agriculture (CSA). This movement links farmers with consumers. A household can subscribe to a farm that delivers produce in season to their door. By fronting the farmer's costs, the household gains less expensive foods in that season. Congregations can support such an agricultural co-op as well. Furthermore, visiting "your" farm can prove both educational and a fun family venture.

## Caring for Our Bodies

First, don't eat mindlessly. Instead, delight in eating well! This could be a household resolution. So often we think that honoring our bodies is an individual activity, but the success of Weight Watchers, Overeaters Anonymous, and a host of other organizations (your church?) suggests that there is a social component involved. In one's household making mindful eating a social event and exploring what this might mean together can help combat individual drifting. (How often I have stood in front of the refrigerator without knowing how I got there.)

Second, find something else to do in your low-resolve hours. No daily activities are more integral to the way we honor our bodies than our eating or drinking. Whether we understand our bodies as friends or enemies, gift or problem, influences how we eat. When I am at low resolve (usually late in the afternoon) I eat foolishly. I do not care for my body, I lose my inhibitions, and I eat or drink carelessly.

Third, change your eating habits. Think about what you are doing when you eat. There are many diets, but the real issue is long-term change. Based on daily exercise and weight control, a diet suggested by Dr. Walter Willett, professor of epidemiology and nutrition at Harvard, recommends whole-grain foods, healthy fats (mono- and polyunsaturated ones), more nuts and legumes, multiple vitamins, and less alcohol. Organic foods add fewer pesticide residues and other contaminants to your body. Eat fewer carbohydrates. Treat your body as a temple!

Fourth, exercise—in a way you enjoy. When we exercise by getting involved in things we enjoy it is easy to feel that our bodies are an integral, irreplaceable part of ourselves. Those endorphins are going; we feel pumped. Our bodies become alert to our limits and our opportunities. We can experience joy in movement. We can enjoy playing with others. Enjoying the pleasures of embodiment means that we can return to our senses. We can become mindful of eating and drinking well. We can eat and drink to our health.

Fifth, cook your own meals, together. Enjoy! Learn about nutrition.

## Quality of Living

First, drink fairly traded coffee, tea, or cocoa. This is a small step, but one that begins to address the issue of how our economic advantages can benefit rather than harm people (see www.equalexchange.com). It acknowledges that our global system is interconnected and begins to take responsibility for redressing it. There is satisfaction in acknowledging your complicity and taking action toward justice. Walk in your community CROP walks (www.churchworldservice.org). Sponsor thirty-hour famines for youth (www.30hourfamine.org). Act!

Second, share with others. Learning to share begins of course with the earliest admonitions of our parents to share with others. We soon realize that sharing is among the experiences that make us genuinely happy. We are dependent on others and our greatest joy comes in relating to them. This begins at home at the supper table when we relate to one another over food. Working at a local rescue mission or food pantry can teach us the joy of hospitality. The foundation of sharing is the fundamental basis of making room for others to instruct, to love, to teach, to learn from, and to embrace us. Take on the task of sharing food as a family or friendship group activity.

Third, practice fasting. Refraining from food allows us a bit of a glimpse of what real hunger is and also allows us to recognize the necessity of food. Fasting enables us as individuals and members of a group to regain appreciation of food as essential, but also gives us a touch of the hunger that millions of people experience every day. Fasting teaches us increased sensitivity to those who are involuntarily hungry and begins to retrain our emotions toward greater gratitude and more compassion for the hungry. We learn that we can do without food for short periods, but that it is not pleasant to do so. Practicing hospitality is thereby enriched and deepened for us.

Fourth, monitor healthful eating for those who are not able to make informed choices. This principle begins with children at home. Steven Gortmaker at the School of Public Health at Harvard suggests that the most powerful technology driving the obesity epidemic is television. There is a correlation between obesity and the number of hours one spends watching TV, not only because of the sedentary nature of TV watching, but also from the impact of advertising on those who are not old enough or wise enough to be discerning about it. Children are also victims of vending machines in schools that sell harmful and unhealthy foods. Monitoring your children's eating habits is a matter of fairness to them.

Fifth, recognize the multitude of people, the amount of soil, and the number of arrangements that go into getting food on your table. This chain is amazing and makes us aware of the solidarity we often unconsciously share with other peoples and the earth. Gratitude and solidarity may issue in table blessing. Our own bounty must make us conscious of our undeserved situation of privilege. Calling this to mind should make us grateful, mindful eaters.

Sixth, pass along appreciation for food to children at home and at school. This can happen in various ways. For example, renowned chef Alice Waters and others have initiated various projects to teach kids how to grow and cook food. The Farm-to-Cafeteria Projects Act authorizes grants to local communities to design a farm-to-cafeteria project tailored to specific needs of farm and school communities. A curriculum at Yale is focused on growing foods from which one college eats completely seasonally, and in another project an overgrown lot has been turned into an organic garden.[10] Churches can have analogous growing projects as part of church school.

Seventh, as a household, join Heifer International, the Foods Resource Bank, your denomination's hunger program, Bread for the World, or any other reputable agency that fights world hunger. Learn with your children about world hunger. Relieve someone's hunger; do something to relieve your own complicity or guilt about having been born in such fortunate circumstances. Investigate what you and your children can do about other people's hunger—and do it. Make hunger and environmental concerns your political agenda. Challenge political candidates about issues of hunger in your community. Let your children see you asking candidates about this.

## A NEW ECONOMIC GLOBALIZATION

We will never return to a pre-Internet world. Instead, we must capitalize on the benefits of globalization and make them work for a food system that is just, sustainable, and delightful. The idea that food is a local product that is best distributed and used locally represents a dramatic modification of the current globalized food system, which is linear and hierarchical rather than interconnected and potentially egalitarian. The present system separates food and eaters from each other. In the process it reinforces household ignorance of what food is; of how to appreciate and buy food; of how to eat sensibly and healthily; and of how to pass along the Christian values of gratitude, enjoyment, and sharing to our children.

The emerging model that focuses on local growing, production, distribution, and buying can be seen in the Food Circles Networking Project, a holistic system (or circle) that connects farmers, eaters, grocers, chefs, and processors, all of whom maintain connections with one another. The best example of local globalization is in Missouri.[11] Its strategy is: (1) to help farm families produce food for local markets; (2) to connect farmers and consumers directly; (3) to strengthen those connections by encouraging community-based processing and distributing; and (4) to work with consumers and communities to encourage consumption of locally grown food. It is easy to imagine how households can participate in this movement or the corresponding one that operates in their own state, county, city, or other community. See www.foodroutes.org/local food/index or www.localharvest.org for your locality.

Individual households must take the lead in demonstrating the power inherent in consumers. We have choices about whom to buy from, which restaurants to support, and how to eat. Ask those who benefit from your patronage where the food comes from and how fresh it is. These are important choices that can offset the sense that the present system of globalization is an irresistible monolith. Making choices can shape us, our children, and friends, allowing us to develop eating practices that are empowering, delightful, resistant, and hospitable. Character formation is essential to detecting and resisting unjust practices that are part of economic globalization.

Considering what and how we eat can awaken us to the religious and moral dimensions of our eating (and living generally). It reconnects the religious and the economic. We are decision makers and we have influence as parents, friends, and consumers. When we view eating as a spiritual practice that is also both economic and empowering, we move toward injecting into the powerful forces of globalization some spiritual alternatives that include the economic and formative power of households. (Fifty percent of the world's assets are connected with the food system. At least 17 percent of employment in the United States is connected to food as well.)

A household movement toward the recognition of the spirituality of eating would redirect globalization toward sustainable and healthy agriculture, empowered households, delightful eating together, and justice for all global peoples. Most importantly, perhaps, it would render globalization a matter of our local choice. It would build the quality of our communities, our churches, and our families.

## QUESTIONS FOR DISCUSSION

1. Can you identify some of the cultural forces of global capitalism that affect the way we eat? How might we become more aware of these influences so that we can change our eating practices and be less complicit in unjust global food systems? How can we take responsibility for our complicity without feeling guilty?
2. Jung talks about the spirituality of eating. How might our eating be informed by delight and sharing? How can we as individuals and communities promote a Christian vision of abundant life? What might change in your life if you were to see eating as a spiritual practice?
3. What would it mean practically if we were to treat our bodies, and all bodies in the world, as temples?

## RESOURCES

### Books and Articles

Cavanagh, John, and Jerry Mander, eds. *Alternatives to Economic Globalization: A Better World Is Possible.* A Report of the International Forum on Globalization. San Francisco: Berrett-Koehler, 2002.

Jung, Shannon. *Food for Life: The Spirituality and Ethics of Eating.* Minneapolis: Fortress Press, 2004.

Pollan, Michael. "The (Agri)Cultural Contradictions of Obesity." *New York Times Magazine,* 12 October 2003, 41–45.

Presbyterian Church (U.S.A.). *We Are What We Eat.* Report approved by the 214th General Assembly (2002). Available from Presbyterian Distribution Service, 1-800-524-2612, refer to PDS #68-600-02-003.

Simon, Arthur. *How Much Is Enough? Hungering for God in an Affluent Culture.* Grand Rapids: Baker, 2003.

Stephen, Diana, ed. "The Agricultural Revolution." *Church & Society,* November/December 2004, 1–96.

### Organizations and Web Sites

Food Circles Networking Project. www.foodcircles.missouri.edu.

Local Harvest. www.localharvest.org.

Bread for the World. www.bread.org.
Community Food Security Coalition. www.foodsecurity.org.
Center for Theology and Land. www.ruralministry.com.
Agricultural Missions, Inc. www.agriculturalmissions.org.

# NOTES

1. Complicity is quite different from guilt and can be less immobilizing. Complicity represents our benefiting from another group of people's suffering without our having done anything to cause that suffering directly. World hunger is such a situation. Guilt is an appropriate response to directly harming another person or group. We recognize our complicity and need to redress it, e.g., by confession, repentance, and change. So, rather than being overwhelmed or simply sweeping our recognition under the rug, we need to take an active role in doing what we can to relieve the suffering of those from whom we are indirectly benefiting.
2. The Worldwatch Institute, *State of the World 2004* (New York: Norton, 2004), 82.
3. U.S. Conference of Catholic Bishops, *For I Was Hungry and You Gave Me Food* (Washington, DC: U.S. Conference of Bishops, 2004).
4. Hilary French and Brian Halweil, "Microbial Migrations," www.oriononline .org/pages/oml-3om/French_Halweil.html (Summer 2001).
5. See Greg Critser, *Fat Land: How Americans Became the Fattest People in the World* (Boston: Houghton Mifflin, 2003), 127–54.
6. Wendell Berry, *Sex, Economy, Freedom & Community* (New York: Pantheon, 1993), quoted in Roger Epp and Dave Whitson, *Writing off the Rural West: Globalization, Governments, and the Transformation of Rural Communities*, (Edmonton: University of Alberta Press, 2001), 301.
7. Pamela Brubaker, *Globalization at What Price?* (Cleveland: Pilgrim Press, 2001), 65.
8. http://www.cfbf.com/programs/yfr/food.cfm, California Farm Bureau Federation, 2/21/05.
9. See *Catholic Rural Life* 46, no. 2 (Spring 2004): 4–7.
10. See *Atlantic Monthly* 294, no. 3 (October 2004).
11. See www.foodcircles.missouri.edu/vision.htm.

# PART TWO
# COMMUNITY STRATEGIES

# Chapter 5

# Holding Corporations Accountable

*Laura Stivers*

Katie Holly had been working at Spray Cotton Mills since 1977. After the passage of the North American Free Trade Agreement (NAFTA) in 1994, many manufacturers in her area and adjoining counties moved to places like Mexico or Asia for cheaper labor costs. Katie was laid off with 140 other textile workers in January 2001. Along with other displaced mill workers, she tried to take advantage of a congressional offer—free tuition and extended unemployment benefits for 18 months for workers displaced by trade—and signed up for classes to earn a high school equivalency diploma. Sixty years old and long out of school, she found studying a struggle and dropped out to work part-time in the kitchen of a nursing home, making half her previous salary. No longer able to keep up on rental payments, she now lives in a motel with her daughter and two grandchildren.[1]

Economic globalization has accelerated the pace of capital movement around the world, causing uprootedness and human displacement on an unprecedented scale. Many are refugees across borders, and others are displaced within their own countries. Between 1999 and 2001, there were 9.9 million displaced workers in the United States alone, up from 7.6 million in the previous Department of Labor survey.[2]

Many displaced workers find new jobs, but they often have to accept pay cuts and lower-quality work or they have to move. Many of us have been exposed to the devastating effects this displacement has on families and communities. In North Carolina where Katie and I live, numerous textile mills and other manufacturers have closed shop, putting the unemployment rate over the last ten years up as high as 11 to 12 percent in some counties.[3] A total of 140,000 manufacturing jobs have been lost in the state of North Carolina between 1994 and 2001.[4] Of course, in the 1950s many of these manufacturing jobs had relocated from New England to the rural South. Thus, while one community gets new jobs when corporations come in, there is no guarantee that that community will not suffer from future capital flight.

Although most of North Carolina's textile mills have relocated in search of cheaper labor, not all businesses are going to low-wage, low-tax countries. In the 1990s two-thirds of cross-border investment was among the twenty-six countries that make up the Organisation for Economic Co-operation and Development.[5] Corporations continue to invest in developing countries, but most of the investment is either in the extraction of raw materials or in the service sector (e.g., hotels, banks), which does not entail labor relocation. Even the majority of business relocations within the United States tend to be in the same metro area and not state to state.[6] Although free trade agreements have facilitated corporate relocation to low-wage countries, most often corporations want locations that offer such amenities as a trained and reliable workforce, good infrastructure, a stable political environment, and proximity to customers and suppliers.

This does not stop corporations, however, from using the scare tactic of relocation to garner public subsidies and dampen labor organizing. Union officials in the United States are routinely warned that their members' jobs will go to Mexico if they demand too much. Whether this threat is true or not, corporations play workforces and production sites off against each other. It is to a corporation's advantage to find the cheapest suppliers of labor. In the global organization of production, capital is not subject to borders, but people are. Thus workers end up competing to offer the cheapest labor with the least social and environmental costs, leading to a downward spiral in all countries, what critic David Korten calls the "new corporate colonialism."[7]

In this new corporate colonialism, the well-being of communities and the environment is being subordinated to the short-term interests of a handful of transnational corporations. I say a *handful* because big corporations are rapidly forming alliances, joint ventures, and mergers that make them economically larger and more powerful than most countries. The rules of global economics are increasingly determined by what some have called the "New Institutional Trinity"—the International Monetary Fund (IMF), the World Bank, and the World Trade Organization (WTO). Critics contend that these international institutions are heavily influenced by corporate power and that many national governments have to bow to pressure from these institutions, thereby limiting their ability to best serve their citizens. I say *short-term* interests because the negative effects (e.g., poverty, displacement of people, environmental destruction) that result when profit takes precedence over the well-being of human communities and the environment are not good for corporations in the long run. Communities around the world are not waiting for corporate interests to figure this out, however. Many are organizing to hold corporations accountable and promote a common good for humans, nonhuman animals, and the environment. It is these communities and the strategies that they employ that are the subject of my discussion in this chapter.

## COMMUNITIES HOLDING CORPORATIONS ACCOUNTABLE

Public policy strategies will be the most effective way to make corporations accountable for their actions, but such policies will be enacted only through community organizing, since national politics in the United States is currently dominated by corporate money. A growing number of local communities and states in our country are actually implementing job quality standards, disclosure, and clawback laws for businesses that receive public subsidies. For example, in Minnesota, companies receiving incentives over $25,000 must report the number of jobs and wages paid every year until their agreement is reached. If the agreement is not met, a clawback law requires payback of the subsidy.

Community organizing efforts have led cities, counties, and states to enact such standards—everyday people are getting involved in holding corporations accountable.[8] One such person is Ana Valenzuela, a native of Mexico living in Los Angeles. Valenzuela was a stay-at-home mom with seven children until the development of the Staples Entertainment Complex threatened her neighborhood. The previous Staples sports arena had displaced residents, increased crime, and left no room for residents to park near their homes. Valenzuela began attending community meetings at the First United Methodist Church, and before she knew it she was involved in negotiating one of our country's largest community benefit agreements (CBA) with Staples Center developers. She was one of the representatives for the newly formed Figueroa Corridor Coalition for Economic Justice, which consisted of twenty-eight community groups, five unions, and over three hundred residents.

CBAs are agreements that communities negotiate directly with developers. They are one example of holding businesses accountable and reversing what some have called the "race to the bottom" of economic globalization. In the Staples case, the community had significant leverage in the negotiations because (1) the developers needed to nail down promised city entitlements before the mayor who supported the project left office, and (2) the location was prime. Valenzuela's community was especially desirable because the goal of the developers was to build an entertainment complex next to the already existing stadium. Communities, like the one in which I live in rural North Carolina, with lots of open land, less developed infrastructure, and lower population often have less leverage in negotiations.

Many of the concessions negotiated in the Staples CBA are standards that could be instituted as public policy at a local, state, or national level.[9] For example, the community negotiated a goal that 70 percent of the jobs in the project would pay a living wage. This is known as a "living wage agreement." The term "living wage" refers here to a rate of hourly pay adjusted to the standard of living that allows full-time workers to live above the poverty line. Tenants of the entertainment complex that participate in the living wage incentive program can receive benefits from funds solicited by the coalition and the developer (from both governmental and private sources). The City of Los Angeles also offers a low-cost way to provide health insurance through a Health Insurance Trust Fund. According to the agreement, tenants are to report annually the percentage of jobs with a living wage as well as those with health insurance, and the coalition then assesses the living wage goal five and ten years from the date of the agreement. Living wage ordinances have been adopted by 130 municipalities across the country as a way to address the increasing number of working people living in poverty.

Another job quality standard in the CBA concerned local hiring and job training. The key target group is individuals whose residence or place of employment was displaced by the Staples Center Project, especially low-income individuals who live in a three-mile radius of the center. The coalition and developer will establish a First Source Referral System through a local community-based job training organization that will coordinate job training and target referrals, and the developer will provide $100,000 in seed funding for the system. Valenzuela's neighbors are hoping that the training programs will land them living wage jobs.

Since the City of Los Angeles already has some public policies that uphold job standards, the coalition was able simply to reinforce these policies. For example, the developer agreed not to lease to any businesses that were declared not to be responsible contractors under the city's Contractor Responsibility Program and also agreed to follow the city's Worker Retention Policy.

Negotiations did not stop there. The coalition also got the developer to agree to develop public parks and open spaces free of charge to all, with the city responsible for maintenance, a welcome alternative to the dangerous streets that Valenzuela's children played in before. Furthermore, residents gained a residential parking program, extra trash pickup around the development, and a traffic liaison to deal with traffic issues connected to the center.

For some of those who were relocated, the developer agreed to provide afford-able housing—20 percent of the five hundred to eight hundred new housing units being built were set aside as affordable in the present and for a minimum of thirty years. Los Angeles, like many other big cities in the United States, has a crisis in housing affordability. Fair market rental rates consume 65 to 83 per-cent of a minimum-wage worker's full-time gross monthly salary, and in the year 2000 the overall vacancy rate in Los Angeles County was 4.7 percent, compared to a national rate of 8 percent.[10] Valenzuela worked hard to make sure that some of the affordable housing units would be reserved for large families. The devel-oper also agreed to work cooperatively with community-based organizations to provide additional affordable housing units and to give some no-interest loans to one or more nonprofit housing developers. Lastly, the developer agreed to meet regularly with the coalition and the city government to assist in finding affordable housing for families that were displaced by the Staples Project.

The process that the Figueroa Corridor Coalition followed to achieve its goals can serve as a model for other communities. Activists from Strategic Actions for a Just Economy (SAJE) and other community groups began the organizing process by creating a base of support. They actually went door to door to figure out what the issues were and what people wanted. They also used popular edu-cation sessions to help build a coalition. All communities seek to have a safe, clean, and healthy environment, but community needs, politics, and member-ship differ. Clearly identifying the particular needs of a community is key to an effective organizing campaign.

Once a base of support was created, meetings were scheduled with the Sta-ples developers. Initially progress was slow. At two scheduled meetings in which two hundred people showed up, the lead Staples representative was a no-show. Luckily, his deputy stepped up and even gave his presentation to the commu-nity in Spanish. From this point on, organizers put in a lot of time; the coalition was young and no one had proposed such a comprehensive platform before. Grassroots groups did research on what had been successful for other commu-nities, and three hundred tenants also had regular meetings.[11] When the nego-tiating team was assembled, organizers with different skills (e.g., housing, environment, jobs) were part of the team as well as a rotating group of four from the tenants, most of whom needed interpreters.

Community Benefit Agreements are not the answer for every community, nor will all corporations respond as positively as Staples did in these circum-stances. What is instructive, however, are the numerous standards available by which communities can hold corporations accountable and the way that communities can effect change by working together. Furthermore, the more organized communities are, the more likely some of these standards can become policy at various governmental levels. The standards set up for the Staples proj-ect are only a sample of the many that can be put in place domestically as well as internationally.[12]

# AN ALTERNATIVE VISION OF ECONOMIC
# GLOBALIZATION

Communities who hold corporations accountable offer a different vision of economic globalization than the neoliberal approach. These communities continue to work from within a capitalist framework, but they insist that businesses that benefit from public subsidy should also be accountable for promoting social and economic justice. In fact, all businesses benefit from various public subsidies in one way or another, either directly through tax credits or economic development subsidies, or indirectly through infrastructure or public schools. To be fair, many businesses pay taxes, but in the last fifty years corporate taxes have decreased, and corporations, especially large ones, have found intricate ways to avoid a majority of taxes. U.S. corporate tax revenues have fallen from an average of 28 percent of federal revenues in the 1950s to 7.4 percent in 2003.[13] Some advocates of neoliberal economic globalization who support reduced government "interference" in the marketplace argue that the nation-state is becoming obsolete because the mobility and liquidity of capital as well as the increase in information technologies are transnational, making it hard for nation-states to regulate. Proponents of alternative visions claim that material and socioeconomic infrastructure is necessary for global economic activity and that this infrastructure is located in particular places and can be regulated by nation-states.[14] Furthermore, advocates for change argue that we have a right to regulate businesses that profit from our tax money.

Two ethical norms promoted by this alternative vision of economic globalization are protection of the common good and rootedness to particular places. In contrast, the neoliberal vision of economic globalization emphasizes the good of large corporations (more specifically shareholders) and mobility of labor and capital.

## Protection of the Common Good

The notion of a common good has been a key ethical norm in Catholic social teachings and can be traced back to Plato's ideal republic and Aristotle's concept of the *polis*. In today's pluralistic world, however, many have critiqued the idea of a common good as monolithic and often oppressive. That is, critics argue that it posits one standard for what is considered "normal" or "moral" in society with that standard benefiting those who are in power. While such an understanding of the common good is oppressive, it is true that communities do agree on some general characteristics or standards that promote a good life for all. For example, in the United States we have publicly supported education, environmental regulations, and labor laws that communities have deemed important for protecting the common good. In the face of increasing global interaction and communication, absent cross-cultural debate about questions of justice, neoliberal economic standards will reign by default.

The emphasis on individualism in neoliberal economics—the idea that society will gain if each individual seeks maximum economic gain—does not promote the long-term welfare of the whole community. In order to work for justice, communities need some shared values that benefit the communities themselves rather than individuals in power. In gathering numerous community groups and residents for dialogue, the Figueroa Coalition allowed a vision of the common good to emerge. This vision included access to basic needs for all, availability of satisfying and useful work, environmental sustainability, and individual and community security. There is no one form of the common good. As the Figueroa Coalition illustrated, identifying the common good is more of a community process than simply looking to a predefined principle.

In addition to holding goods in common, communities must allow diversity of cultures and lifestyles to avoid exclusivity and tyranny. Such openness requires more than tolerance of differences, however. Affluent communities often tolerate communities different from themselves without true respect and without changing structural inequities in distribution of resources and access to power. Simple tolerance of diversity does not provide a sufficient foundation for the institutional changes that must happen to promote the long-term welfare of all communities. Solidarity and justice are necessary foundations for promoting a common good. Solidarity entails a community of people acting together with true respect for each person's dignity.[15] For solidarity to promote justice, analysis and reconfiguring of power relations is necessary so that those most often exploited or marginalized can participate in shaping policies that affect their community. Having community members like Valenzuela play a key role in the CBA negotiating process was crucial to the Figueroa Coalition's success. Such participation ensured that actual needs were addressed, neighborhood diversity was affirmed, and community members were empowered.

The Christian tradition holds that we are created in God's image and that justice is rooted in the very being of God. The dignity of persons is rooted in this concept of the image of God. Furthermore, individuals do not live in isolation, but are interconnected. If we are to take seriously the dignity of persons, economic and other social institutions should empower, not exploit, humans. In short, social and economic justice are central to the common good. The goodness of creation extends beyond humans to nonhuman animals and all of nature. Thus ecological sustainability is also part of the common good. Justice is connected to the dignity and integrity of God's creation. The Christian tradition calls us to solidarity with those humans who are marginalized by or made powerless in our economic institutions, and with other species and ecosystems that are being exploited. Being in solidarity means working with others to create economic institutions that promote human dignity and environmental sustainability. Promoting justice is not sweet and easy, however. It can require standing up to powerful interests as the Figueroa Corridor Coalition did. Having some standards of a common good helped the coalition be in solidarity with those who would be affected most negatively by the development project.

Although the coalition was representing diverse constituencies, they worked together to address common needs in the community. The process followed a bottom-up model by listening to the three hundred residents of the area and continuing to keep them involved with representation on the negotiating team. In contrast, neoliberal economic globalization imposes a top-down model, one size fits all, that does not prioritize on a long-term basis the different needs of particular communities. Tom Friedman, in his best-selling book *The Lexus and the Olive Tree*, calls this model the "Golden Straightjacket" in which the economic decision making is handed over from local communities and the state to the free market.[16] In other words, all economic policies are geared toward opening up markets for transnational capital.

## Rootedness to Particular Places

The notion of rootedness to place is also not a new concept. Rootedness to a particular place is a central promise of God to the people of Israel in biblical times, and Aristotle held that every substance is place-bound and in fact has its own "proper place." The idea of "place" has gained new attention from theorists today due to increasing displacement from economic globalization. Philosopher Iris Marion Young writes:

> Today corporate capital is homeless. . . . Mergers, interlocking directorships, holding companies, and the dispersion of ownership through securities and stock market speculation mean that political and economic power is dislodged from place. Fast as a satellite signal, capital travels from one end of a continent to the other, from one end of the world to the other. Its direction depends on the pull of profit, and its directors rarely consider how its movement may affect local economies.[17]

Although capital moves freely, people are not uprooted so easily. Yet global capitalism increasingly assumes the "transnationalization of labor,"[18] that people can be easily transferred from one place to another or can simply be replaced. Numerous people are being exiled and uprooted, living "out of place" to go where the jobs are. While most Americans are concerned about the outsourcing of jobs from this country overseas, many workers in developing countries have routinely had to move away from traditional lands and families in order to follow the jobs.

As Americans we have ambivalence about rootedness to places. Since World War II, mobility has been an elite social value connected to money and education. Staying in one place has meant backwardness or lack of choice, the lot of the poor and uncultured. Mobility is a freedom of modern life and staying in one place can be boring, but there is a difference between voluntary and coerced mobility. In other words, the jet-mobile CEO has more control and autonomy in relation to global mobility than the undocumented migrant from Mexico. Yet even the elite have some need for rootedness. Moving from job to job, sometimes hundreds of miles away, can have negative effects on our sense of home and local involvement in the community.

Much of the literature on rootedness to place is found in environmental studies, influenced by Aldo Leopold's *land ethic* in which he makes a case for really knowing and being connected to the land and ecological community of one's "place."[19] Although the literature tends to emphasize rural or wilderness areas rather than cities, all groups have a sense of place, and cities have ecological communities as well. Furthermore, our sense of place depends on relationships and memories, not only on physical features. Thus our belonging to a place involves both a connection to specific places and networks of stable relationships. Although many of the residents of Los Angeles who live around the Staples Development are recent immigrants, they create new memories and relationships in this place.

Places can, however, be contested realities and ought not be romanticized as idyllic. Places are experienced and interpreted differently by different groups and cannot be separated from issues of dominance and exclusion. Each social and ethnic group in the Figueroa Corridor has different understandings and relationships to their "home" in Los Angeles. The Staples Development could have further marginalized the already displaced migrants and other community members and could have caused divisiveness and violence among various groups. Instead these groups came together in solidarity and worked together to create a place that is "home" to all.

The stories of a place evoke different memories. They are layered as a text is layered with meaning. Unfortunately, neoliberal economic globalization can displace people, breaking the lineage of memory associated with their home-place. Equally destructive is the homogenizing consumerism of fast-food restaurants and big box retail that dominates and erases the particularities of a place. When flying to the Netherlands recently, the first thing I saw from the plane window was the infamous "Golden Arches." When places are homogenized, historical connections are destroyed and narratives of certain groups are ignored. Communities working together for justice in a particular geographical area, as the coalition did, can ensure the voices of the marginalized are heard, empowering a heterogeneous vision of place.

Rootedness to place is not simply a social issue, but also a spiritual and theological one. Belonging to a place means being intimate with the people, land, and institutions of one's community and region. Spiritual wholeness depends on such intimacy. Such intimacy and belonging can be an important foundation for spiritual well-being as people often experience the divine in deep connection with human community and/or nature. Furthermore, such interconnection can be an impetus for solidarity with one another and creation, in which communities organize together to promote the well-being of all, especially the most marginalized and exploited.

Some theologians have argued that Christianity has been a religion of pilgrimage and dislocation rather than placement. Human social places have been viewed with suspicion—Augustine's "City of God" or eternal fulfillment takes precedence over the human city. Christian feminist theologians and others have more recently argued for a God who is "embodied" and who is intimately connected to particular places. Theologian Sallie McFague argues for a model of God as the body of creation and the universe. Embracing the earth as part of the body of God is the first step toward responsibility and love of the earth and its many bodies.[20] An embodied God is seen in Jesus' healing of the sick and engagement with those who were considered unclean in society (e.g., lepers, women, tax collectors).

The community organizing of the Figueroa Corridor Coalition for Economic Justice promotes the idea of rootedness to a particular place. Community residents are standing up for their right to remain in their neighborhoods and not simply be uprooted in the name of urban renewal. They are also seeking the means for thriving communities, embodied as places, where people can afford housing, have health care, work at decent jobs, and socialize in open spaces. In contrast, neoliberal economic globalization pays no attention to the distinctiveness of particular communities and is not concerned with whether communities stay intact. Unless they are held accountable to particular communities, most corporations are concerned only with their shareholders' bottom line.

## STANDARDS SUPPORTIVE OF THE COMMON GOOD AND ROOTEDNESS TO PLACE

The standards that the coalition negotiated promote a common good for the community and aim to keep people rooted in a place. A living wage for residents of the community will put more money in their pockets, allowing families to afford basic needs and increasing money spent in the community. Good-paying jobs on the lower end is one step to closing the gap between the rich and poor. A living wage lessens job turnover, which is detrimental to both families and businesses. Most importantly, a living wage better promotes human dignity, a prerequisite to a healthy community.

Hiring locally and offering affordable housing with priority given to low-income residents and those displaced from the Staples Stadium will be the most helpful strategy for keeping people rooted in a place. Without the local hiring standard, residents would simply be excluded from economic development, and without low-income housing, residents would be priced out of the area. In particular, low-income communities must be vigilant in protecting themselves against corporate exploitation, marginalization, and displacement. They cannot do it alone, however. It takes solidarity with other groups as well.

Attention to the environment in the CBA is also a form of protecting the common good and key to residents feeling a connection to their place. Accessible parks and open space allow residents to have a connection to the land and to one another. Playgrounds, community fairs, and farmers' markets all facilitate community building. The more the connection, the more rooted people are to a place and the more likely they are to work together to create stable and thriving communities.

Holding corporations accountable is beneficial not only to local communities and to the environment, but to the corporations themselves. Businesses increasingly need a stable, educated workforce, good infrastructure, and markets to buy their goods and services. Simply looking out for the good of shareholders while ignoring the good of communities will, in the long run, be a losing option. We are no longer in the era when "What is good for GM is good for America." It is time to hold corporations accountable to particular communities and particular places. Only then will economic globalization cease to be a "race to the bottom."

## QUESTIONS FOR DISCUSSION

1. Find out some of the ways in which your local city/county/state government has offered incentives to corporations to relocate to your area. Does the government hold these corporations accountable in some way (i.e., hiring quotas, living wages, environmental sensitivity, local hiring, affordable housing)? How might you and your local congregation get involved in promoting corporate accountability? Have you thought about joining a coalition of groups to negotiate CBAs with corporations?

2. Research your own local community to see how the working poor are faring. Is there a living wage ordinance in your city/county? Is affordable housing an issue for people in your community? How might you and your congregation get involved in advocating for the working poor?

3. What are important aspects of a common good in your community? How might groups within your community work together to promote the common good and how might your community work with other communities to avoid competing against one another in attracting corporate investment? How can your congregations and communities make sure that all people have a place that they can feel rooted and at home?

# RESOURCES

## Books and Articles

Danaher, Kevin, ed. *Corporations Are Gonna Get Your Mama: Globalization and the Downsizing of the American Dream.* Monroe, ME: Common Courage Press, 1997.

Derber, Charles. *Corporation Nation: How Corporations Are Taking Over Our Lives and What We Can Do About It.* New York: St. Martin's Press, 2000.

Korten, David C. *The Post-Corporate World: Life After Capitalism.* West Hartford, CT: Kumarian, 1999.

———. *When Corporations Rule the World.* West Hartford, CT: Kumarian, 1995.

LeRoy, Greg. *The Great American Jobs Scam: Corporate Tax Dodging and the Myth of Job Creation.* San Francisco: Berrett-Koehler, 2005.

Mokhiber, Russel, and Robert Weisman. *Corporate Predators: The Hunt for Mega-Profits and the Attack on Democracy.* Monroe, ME: Common Courage Press, 1999.

## Organizations and Web Sites

Good Jobs First. www.goodjobsfirst.org.

Program on Corporations, Law and Democracy. www.poclad.org.

Working for America Institute. www.workingforamerica.org.

Reclaim Democracy. www.reclaimdemocracy.org.

Employment Policies Institute. www.livingwage.org.

Center for Corporate Policy. www.corporatepolicy.org.

# NOTES

1. Karin Rives, "No End in Sight to N.C. Job Losses," *The News & Observer,* 18 August 2002; see http://www.newsobserver.com/292/story/229031.html.

2. Displaced Workers Summary. United States Department of Labor (21 August 2002); http://ww.bls.gov/news.release/disp.nr0.htm.

3. Civilian labor force estimates for 1995 to 2005, North Carolina Employment Security Commission; http://eslmi40.esc.state.nc.us/ThematicLAUS/clfasp/CLFaasy.asp.

4. Rives, "No End in Sight."

5. Hans-Peter Martin and Harald Schumann, trans. Patrick Camiller, *The Global Trap: Globalization and the Assault on Prosperity and Democracy* (London: Zed, 1996), 151.

6. Greg LeRoy, "Eight Concrete Ways to Curtail the Economic War Among the States," Good Jobs First. Conference paper for "Reigning in the Competition for Capital," Humphrey Institute of Public Affairs, University of Minnesota, Minneapolis (February 2–27, 2004):12.

7. David C. Korten, *When Corporations Rule the World* (West Hartford, CT: Kumarian, 1995), 252.

8. Lee Romney, "Staples Plan Spotlights Invisible Communities," *Los Angeles Times,* 2 June 2001.

9. For a full description of the concessions see "LA Sports and Entertainment District Agreement" on the Strategic Actions for a Just Economy Web site: www.saje.net.

10. Los Angeles Coalition to End Hunger and Homelessness fact sheet; http://www.lacehh.org/factsheet2003A.htm.
11. See Andrea Gibbons and Gilda Haas, "Redefining Redevelopment: Participatory Research for Equity in the Los Angeles Figueroa Corridor," Figueroa Corridor Coalition for Economic Justice (September 2002) at www.saje.net.
12. See the Good Jobs First Web site for information on standards various cities and states have put in place: www.goodjobsfirst.org.
13. Joel Friedman, "The Decline of Corporate Income Tax Revenues," Center on Budget and Policy Priorities, October 2003.
14. See Saskia Sassen, *Globalization and Its Discontents* (New York: New Press, 1998).
15. David Hollenbach, S.J., *The Common Good and Christian Ethics* (Cambridge, UK: Cambridge University Press, 2002), 67–71, 137–70.
16. Thomas L. Friedman, *The Lexus and the Olive Tree* (New York: Anchor, 2000).
17. Iris Marion Young, *Justice and the Politics of Difference* (Princeton: Princeton University Press, 1990), 242.
18. Sassen, *Globalization and Its Discontents*, xxx.
19. Aldo Leopold, *A Sand County Almanac* (Oxford: Oxford University Press, 1949).
20. Sallie McFague, *The Body of God: An Ecological Theology* (Minneapolis: Fortress Press, 1993).

# Chapter 6

# Engaging Environmental Justice

*Carlton Waterhouse*

Globalization produces a variety of effects—some desirable, many not. The undesirable effects, what I call the collateral damage accompanying globalization, include economic displacement, ecological destruction, and political estrangement. Economic displacement means that workers no longer have employment opportunities rooted in the life of their local communities. The growth and "development" associated with globalization are often based on the destruction of ecosystems and habitats. Furthermore, development and growth almost always mean the expansion of consumer culture and the proportionate increase in pollution and pollution sources. Politically, globalization means the increased influence of economic entities such as large corporations on local politicians as these entities expand their power and influence into additional markets.

Globalization raises a variety of specific environmental justice concerns across the world. In central India, American-based multinational companies ensure profits by selling genetically engineered seed that produces a "seedless" harvest; thus farmers will not be able to save some of the crop to plant as seeds the next year as is their traditional practice. International oil companies with interests in Nigeria gain consistent profits by drilling in the oil-rich region of the Niger Delta, while the traditional fishing and farming economy has been destroyed by oil-based pollution. Native American families for whom fish from America's Great Lakes are a dietary staple face a high risk of brain damage for their current and future children due to high mercury levels in the fish, which have been contaminated by mercury dumped into the lakes. Despite the risks to them and other subsistence populations, protective mercury standards for American industry will not take effect until 2018 based on the reasoning that most of the fish Americans eat is imported from other countries without mercury protection standards. Each of these examples represents a strand in the web of environmental injustices facing many communities. Cutting through these strands poses significant challenges for local communities—challenges some communities face daily.

Environmental justice in the United States has been broadly defined by the Environmental Protection Agency (EPA) as "the fair treatment and meaningful involvement of all people regardless of race, color, national origin, or income with respect to the development, implementation, and enforcement of environmental laws, regulations, and policies." Communities primarily comprised of people of color or poor whites beset by multiple pollution sources and political neglect are the majority of those, nationally and internationally, who face environmental injustices. Despite overwhelming odds, limited resources, and endemic race, class, and gender discrimination, many of these communities display valuable attributes of communal well-being in addressing environmental and social injustices. The fortitude and strength of these communities represent the heart of the environmental justice movement. In this chapter, I suggest that these communities possess communal virtues associated with a good "communal" life. These virtues comprise the character needed for communities to resist the ultimate threat of globalization: communal dissolution, alienation, and death.

One such community that is dealing with the effects of globalization, specifically environmental injustice, is in the city and county of Spartanburg, located in the upper northwestern region of South Carolina. Arkwright and Forest Park, two neighborhoods within the city and the county, are situated beyond the principal section of downtown. At one time they formed a single community, but over the years they became divided. These neighborhoods, which are overwhelmingly African American, suffered roughly 10 percent unemployment and 25 percent of their members lived below federal poverty levels. North of these neighborhoods the downtown section of Spartanburg underwent an economic revival through a multimillion-dollar community development effort, yet this development did not alleviate the economic depression and environmental contamination in the Arkwright/Forest Park community.

After living with significant environmental problems for decades, the neighborhoods took a new direction in 1998 when they formed a community-based environmental justice organization named ReGenesis. Through the community's efforts, residents have negotiated a settlement with the former owner of a fertilizer plant that had polluted the area, the EPA has begun federal cleanup action, and the city has enlisted residents' help in identifying other parties responsible for the pollution at the closed dump site. Moreover, the community received several federal and private foundation grants for community development projects. For example, a grant from the U.S. Department of Health and Human Services facilitated construction and operation of the ReGenesis Community Health Center.

## COMMUNAL VIRTUES

My primary concern in this chapter is to identify and promote ways that we can share our lives together on earth. The idea of collective or communal virtue is much less common than that of individual virtue. Although families, groups, organizations, and communities are often characterized as sharing common traits, describing those traits as virtues is fairly rare. Nonetheless, identifying some communal traits as virtues reminds us of the deep potential of our communities for well-being and the ability to access that potential by certain habits of action.

Virtues are usually defined as commendable character traits manifested in habitual action. For example, the virtue of honesty is not found in someone who tells the truth only occasionally. The honest person's actions arise from a relatively fixed and firm character. Furthermore, the honest person will typically have a disposition to feel and act in an honest way and feel an aversion to dishonesty. Virtues are also the character traits that it is good for everyone to have, that is, they are morally or socially valued. Communal virtues refer to character traits that communities exhibit. Communal virtue cannot be viewed in the same way as individual virtue, since communities do not have unchangeable dispositions per se, but communities do habitually embody socially valued character traits, as I will show in this chapter.

Virtue is distinct from a strategy or a tactic intended to produce a particular result in a particular set of circumstances. In the civil rights movement, love stood out as a virtue fostered by Dr. Martin Luther King Jr. and other leaders. In contrast, nonviolent direct action represented a strategy for challenging Jim Crow segregation rooted in the Gandhian philosophy of nonviolence. The Southern Christian Leadership Conference (SCLC), under the guidance of Dr. King, encouraged people to embrace love in their relationships with others as a way of living each day. Nonviolent direct action, however, was primarily taught to persons engaging in the various campaigns undertaken by the SCLC as well as the Student Non-Violent Coordinating Committee (SNCC).

The most obvious distinction between the virtue of love and the tactic of nonviolent direct action is its applicability. Love, as a virtue, has a universal applicability that transcends language, culture, and nationality. It can speak to the human experience across a vast range of circumstances. "Love never fails," according to the apostle Paul (1 Corinthians 13:8 NIV). It produces something in the lover, is a witness to the Divine in the person loved, and testifies to a deeper reality for everyone else. The success of nonviolent direct action in the civil rights movement by and large depended on violent opposition, television coverage, and friendly courts. SCLC and SNCC experienced a significant failure in Albany, Georgia, in part because Laurie Pritchett, the sheriff there, studied Dr. King's past campaigns and treated the activists with dignity and kindness while jailing them for breaking the Jim Crow laws. Consequently, Albany generated very little national attention. In contrast, Bull Connor responded to civil rights activists with hatred and venom, turning water hoses and police dogs on both adults and children. Few people know about SCLC and SNCC's failure in Albany. However, people all over the world have seen television footage from the Birmingham campaign. A strategy that works under one set of circumstances can be a complete failure under another set of circumstances. Nonviolent direct action failed in Albany for the same reason that it succeeded in Birmingham: In Albany the sheriff did not respond with brutality, so there was little media attention. In Birmingham Bull Connor's brutality brought media attention, which raised national pressure for change.

I am not implying here that strategies are bad or that they should be avoided. Strategies are important and they need to be developed by each community working toward social change. But developing strategies is not the starting place for social change. I want to emphasize the importance of communally negotiated and shared virtues and the role that they play in guiding communities as they develop particular strategies and approaches to environmental injustices. In order to be effective, strategies need to reflect the core virtues practiced by a community. Each community that works for social change and social justice must attend to establishing, recognizing, and practicing a common set of shared virtues. It is only from these virtues that practical and effective strategies will arise.

As a result of my experience observing and working with communities pursuing environmental justice, I am convinced that the way communities respond to environmental injustices profoundly affects the future health and well-being of those communities. Some strategies that communities use may offer temporary or limited success at the cost of the community's ultimate well-being. In some cases communities fragment and are overcome by internal strife. Other communities may lose hope and give up because of failed strategies or excessive apathy. I believe that communal virtue offers a deep resource for communities. It enables them to replenish over time and renews their human spirit. A commitment to communal virtues enables community members to weather the ups and downs associated with activism by focusing on community-sustaining practices in the wake of short-term victories and defeats. In too many cases, despair and surrender follow what should be only temporary setbacks. In the examples that follow, I identify communal virtues that work to the good of the communities that manifest them as they struggle with significant environmental injustice. These virtues help sustain these communities and inspire others who come in contact with them toward more virtuous action.

The virtues associated with good communal life that I draw upon in this chapter come from Christian Scripture and African American culture. While space does not permit full development of the notion of a good communal life, I offer a brief account of three communal virtues—collective work and responsibility, purpose, and unity—as shown in the practices of one community that faced grave environmental injustices. My contention is that these virtues work toward a form of long-term communal happiness. My hope is that by examining the work of one successful community, other communities might gain insight into how to think about, develop, and prioritize their own communal virtues.

While justification of Scripture is not necessary in a book written for the Christian community, the use of virtues drawn from the African American celebration of Kwanzaa requires some background information. Dr. Maulana Karenga created Kwanzaa in an effort to help reconnect African Americans to their African heritage. Through his studies of African cultures, Dr. Karenga found significant similarities in the communal virtues of many African peoples. He created a holiday celebration that reflected traditional celebrations common to West African cultures for the firstfruits of the harvest. The centerpiece of the Kwanzaa celebration is the Nguzo Saba or the seven principles of Kwanzaa: *umoja, kujichaqulia, ujima, ujamaa, nia, kuumba,* and *imani*; respectively, unity, self-determination, collective work and responsibility, cooperative economics, purpose, creativity, and faith. While these virtues or principles are specifically applied to African American communal development and culture by Karenga, I believe that they have far-reaching appeal across cultures and communities confronting environmental injustices. These principles also represent shared virtues in historical and contemporary Christian communities. Here I focus on *ujima, nia,* and *umoja*.

## COMMUNAL VIRTUE IN ACTION

### Virtue of Collective Work and Responsibility

Dr. Karenga defines *ujima* as follows: "To build and maintain our community together and make our brother's and sister's problems our problems by solving them together."[1] Christian Scripture provides numerous examples of collective work and responsibility taking place and being encouraged within communities. In the Old Testament, the collective efforts undertaken by Jews to rebuild the temple and the walls of Jerusalem in the books of Ezra and Nehemiah come to mind. In his Letter to the Romans, Paul directs community members to work collectively as a body toward their common purposes in Christ. Despite different gifts and abilities, Paul encourages them as a community to use their own gifts responsibly while valuing the gifts that others contribute. Moreover, Paul calls this community to recognize the interconnectedness of the work they do and their shared responsibility for one another's well-being.

Communities beset by multiple environmental hardships also suffer from economic and political marginalization. Limited economic opportunities for community members provide an important background to the political marginalization and environmental stressors experienced by many of these communities. Under these circumstances, community members must confront discouragement, apathy, and antagonisms among themselves. The additional burden that poverty brings to some communities can create an overwhelming sense of helplessness to produce change. Nonetheless, communities confronting environmental injustice sometimes undergo the education, organization, and politicization necessary to confront corporate and government policies that discount the value of their participation. When this occurs, these communities serve as important examples of how communities can resist external forces of marginalization and alienation.

Like residents in many other communities facing environmental injustices, Arkwright/Forest Park community members were exposed to multiple pollution sources in close proximity to their homes. The roughly 4,700 community residents live within one mile of a forty-acre abandoned fertilizer plant, a thirty-acre closed municipal landfill, and an operating chemical plant. In addition, an operating textile manufacturer, concrete production businesses, and other commercial and industrial facilities are located nearby. Consequently, community residents complained of truck traffic, odors, smoke, and high cancer and infant mortality rates. These problems are what led to the formation of ReGenesis.

ReGenesis flowed out of the efforts of community resident Harold Mitchell to involve community members in addressing environmental and other problems facing the community. From the beginning, Mitchell met with community members individually and in groups to solicit their input and involvement. He first met with them during his personal investigation of pollution problems in the community. After examining government records of complaints and other issues related to local pollution sources, Mitchell shared his findings in a town meeting that led to an EPA reevaluation of contamination in the area.

ReGenesis operates collectively. It holds regular meetings with community members to inform them of developments, report on ongoing projects, and gain input on how to proceed in efforts to revitalize the community. Structurally, the organization functions through Mitchell, the executive director; a board of directors made up of community residents; and its fourteen hundred members. In practice, the community extended its collective work and responsibility ideal by establishing the ReGenesis Environmental Justice Partnership. The partnership boasts over 124 partners including nonprofit organizations, private sector businesses, governmental agencies, and others. Perhaps the most important feature of the partnership is the core steering committee—ReGenesis, the City of Spartanburg, and Spartanburg County. This committee shares responsibility for planning meetings for the larger partnership and community forums to keep community members informed and involved. Meetings are frequently held in conjunction with one another and include federal, state, and local government representatives as well as technical consultants to address questions.

Despite the collective ideal and practices of the community, initial dealings with city and county bureaucracies were a real challenge. After inviting the city's community development coordinator to a community meeting to clarify the roles played by different government offices, community members gained a more thorough understanding of the process and were able to coordinate better with the local bureaucracy. Likewise, government representatives learned more about the community's needs and desires and thus improved their interaction with the community and with one another.

The community's consistent demonstration of collective work and responsibility has produced recurring benefits for them, the surrounding area, and everyone inspired by their story. Residents themselves have been able to move from an attitude of complacency about their community's future and their ability to improve it to one of hopeful anticipation. Beyond a sense of hopefulness about the community's future, residents can point to meaningful progress in addressing both their environmental and community revitalization concerns. Through the community's efforts, residents have received a settlement with the former owner of the fertilizer plant, the EPA has begun federal cleanup action, and the city has enlisted residents' help in identifying other parties responsible for the pollution at the closed dump site. Moreover, the community has received $200,000 worth of federal cleanup grants through EPA's Brownfields program; a $225,000 Weed and Seed grant from the Department of Justice; a $230,000 Ford Foundation grant; a $1.2 million U.S. Senate appropriation for transportation development; some $6 million in redevelopment grants from the City and County of Spartanburg; and the construction and operation of the ReGenesis Community Health Center built with a $552,000 grant from the U.S. Department of Health and Human Services. In its first three months, the health center treated over 2,400 patients, providing dental care, mental health care, counseling, health screenings, services for environmental related ailments, traditional health care for the insured and uninsured, and an in-house pharmacy.

Jim Palmer, EPA regional administrator, observed: "What sets the effort in Spartanburg apart from others in the country is the willingness of different groups, including area businesses, and local governments to work together."[2]

The collective effort did not come naturally, however. It resulted from communal education and outreach to community members and others with responsibility for the community's well-being. Interviewees from the area made the following comments about the process:

> In the beginning there was no cooperative spirit. Early on the community was not happy with the current state of affairs.

> Harold made the first step reaching out . . . saying, "We want you to be involved," and asked for our input.

> The community group is the driver and the most important partners are the local government partners.

> Now we actually have federal, state, local, and community all sitting down talking about the same issue. Previously only adversarial stances were taken. . . . [Now] everyone more or less shares the same vision.

> This has been a real coming of age for people in the community. So much face-to-face contact. It caused local people to recognize the extent of resources available.[3]

During forums held in 2000 to address community revitalization, community members identified objectives related to their community revitalization goal. Of the objectives selected, two of them best highlight the community's solid commitment to collective work and responsibility. Specifically, the community committed to "work together to build local commitment and plan to develop partnerships at the local, state, and federal level," and to "generate recommendations to ensure community involvement as well as short- and long-term development strategies."

The community's commitment to and expression of collective work and responsibility influenced others to embrace it. Mayor William Barnett of Spartanburg and other local governmental officials were motivated to break through the bureaucracy dividing city and county responsibilities to better address concerns of the community residents. Cory Fleming, the reporter who interviewed Barnett for an article discussing the partnership formed between the community, the city, and the county government, described Barnett's perspective:

> While the circumstances leading to the formation of the partnership were on a few occasions less than pleasant, he feels that the experience has encouraged improved teamwork among county staff, built stronger relationships between city and county government, and allowed for tremendous professional and personal growth for many of the stakeholders in the partnership. . . . "Probably, the most important thing we've learned is how to approach these challenges collectively."[4]

Barnett goes on to point out that the leadership for the partnership efforts came from Mitchell, who focused on getting the neighborhood residents engaged in improving their community.

The consistent and faithful leadership by Mitchell represents a vital component of this community's success. However, Mitchell's greatest contribution seems to have been his ability to inspire the community and its partners to embrace a collective approach to resolve the community's environmental and other problems. As a result, community members collectively developed a vision for the future of their community, and found partners to help them make that vision a reality. Mitchell wrote:

> For years I felt people needed an example of a solution for impacted communities rather than the confrontational verbiage that had been so much a part of the past standoffs. The longevity of these tactics is a testament to their effectiveness at an earlier time in the environmental justice movement. But today's climate is not conducive to strategies that create divides between and among the segments of our society that must work together to foster equitable solutions to broadly based community problems.[5]

His words, like those of Mayor Barnett, highlight the commitment of ReGenesis and the entire community to work collectively to revitalize their community. They also show the influence that commitment has had on others.

## Virtue of Purpose

Although collective work and responsibility represents the strongest virtue of the Arkwright/Forest Park community, the success of the community would not have been possible without at least two other communal virtues: purpose and unity. Communities facing intense economic depression and widespread environmental pollution also contend with crime, minimal social and commercial services, and apathy. Just thinking about the need to confront such a range of serious problems overwhelms most people, paralyzing them so that they do not take action. To move beyond that paralysis, the community needed a purpose to focus on that allowed them to become engaged. The cleanup and revitalization of their neighborhoods provided that focus. From the beginning of ReGenesis, the community began to embrace a purpose that sustained and inspired all of their efforts. That commitment to and demonstration of communal purpose played a critical role in the community's well-being.

Karenga offers the following in defining *nia*: "To make our collective vocation the building and developing of our community."[6] As with collective work and responsibility, Christian Scripture provides abundant examples of communities uniting around a common purpose. In the book of Nehemiah, Nehemiah discusses the efforts of Jews to rebuild the walls of Jerusalem that were destroyed by the Babylonians:

> Then I said to them, "You see the trouble we are in, how Jerusalem lies in ruins with its gates burned. Come, let us rebuild the wall of Jerusalem, so that we may no longer suffer disgrace." I told them that the hand of my God had been gracious upon me, and also the words that the king had spoken to me. Then they said, "Let us start building!" So they committed themselves to the common good. (Nehemiah 2:17–18)

In this text, Nehemiah has traveled to Jerusalem to help rebuild the walls of the city. He solicited the support of local community leaders in the effort. With this purpose in mind, leaders and residents came together to rebuild the walls of the city and to restore their community.

ReGenesis and the community residents in Spartanburg, like the ancient citizens of Jerusalem, committed themselves to the common purpose of building up their community. Their commitment to a common purpose is displayed in the final objective established by community members for the community revitalization forums already mentioned. It was simply to "achieve a beneficial revitalization for the Arkwright/Forest Park community." This basic shared understanding of a common purpose highlights the second of the three communal virtues characterizing the Arkwright/Forest Park community.

## Virtue of Unity

The third communal virtue of unity is illustrated by the principle *umoja*: "To strive for and maintain unity in the family, [and] community."[7] This principle coincides with guidance the apostle Paul gave the Christian community in Corinth: "Now I appeal to you, brothers and sisters, by the name of our Lord Jesus Christ, that all of you be in agreement and that there be no divisions among you, but that you be united in the same mind and the same purpose" (1 Corinthians 1:10). Paul appeals for unity among the members of the Christian community in Corinth and asserts that they need to be united in a common vision and a common purpose.

In the environmental justice movement, the division and fragmentation of affected communities can serve as significant obstacles to success in striving for a clean environment. The division within communities often prevents effective communication and the development of collective goals. This fragmentation provides convenient reasons for government inaction and corporate neglect. Environmental officials working with communities at odds are forced to spend time dealing with community infighting that would be better spent serving the community's environmental and other needs. Community fragmentation can also erode opportunities for partnership and assistance from businesses or nonprofit organizations unwilling to venture into the uncertainty that fractured communities represent. Without unity among the community members and a common commitment that the work that is being done is for the common good, collective work and responsibility becomes impossible. Instead of collaborative interaction, residents work at cross-purposes that may burn them out and discourage others from getting involved. Likewise, in the absence of unity a common sense of purpose may elude residents, who instead of focusing on a common vision focus on overcoming their "opposition."

Residents of the Arkwright and Forest Park neighborhoods had many opportunities for division during the past several years. With the formation of ReGenesis, the two neighborhoods began functioning as one community, although previously their interaction had been limited. Residents could easily have seen their interests differing based on where they lived or what they perceived as the greatest problem. Likewise, residents could have divided over Mitchell's leadership. The decision to work with the city and the county also served as a critical juncture for the community. At that time, the community could easily have split over the decision to adopt a collaborative relationship with local government. Countless other legitimate and spurious causes could have driven a wedge between members of this community. However, this community stood unified in all its endeavors. In working with government representatives, corporate actors, and other nonprofit organizations, community residents consistently maintained their commitment to act in unity.

This commitment to united action was fostered by and encouraged through the collective approach adopted by Mitchell and ReGenesis from the beginning. Mitchell's initial involvement and engagement of community members followed by ReGenesis's consistent meetings and forums involving the community in planning and decision making all discouraged fragmentation and division. In the same way, the community's decision to focus their efforts on a common purpose and goal facilitated their collective action and continued unity. As a result, the residents accepted responsibility for collectively working to bring about the cleanup and revitalization of their community.

## CONCLUSION

In light of the virtues consistently shown by this community, the large number of grants and the amount of funding they secured is completely understandable. The community's character draws the attention and earns the respect of friends and foes alike. Academics, business leaders, government officials, senators, and congressional representatives have all taken note of the Arkwright/Forest Park community. Their story serves as inspiration to other overwhelmed communities across the country that also confront environmental and social injustices on a daily basis. Beyond its strategy and tactics, the community is known for its character. In addition to the number of grants received and the cleanup actions undertaken, community members experience an improved quality of life because of the work of ReGenesis and their expression of these virtues. By working together toward a shared vision for their community, residents immediately improved their quality of life. Once that occurred, the residents had tapped a powerful source of human well-being to help sustain them and countless others who hear their story. Ultimately, their embrace of communal virtue serves as a bright beacon to other local communities around the world facing the threat of economic depression, environmental injustice, and political marginalization posed by globalization.

## QUESTIONS FOR DISCUSSION

1. Become familiar with issues of environmental injustice in your local community and state. What concerns have been raised? How might your congregation get involved in supporting environmental justice in your area?
2. How might your local community or congregation exhibit communal virtues in addressing issues and problems posed by economic globalization? How could fostering communal virtue provide a deeper foundation and impetus for change?
3. Some people place concern for human beings at odds with concern for the environment. How are the two connected in your community and how can your local community or congregation address social and environmental justice simultaneously?

## RESOURCES

### Books and Articles

Bullard, Robert D. *Dumping in Dixie: Race, Class, and Environmental Quality.* Boulder, CO: Westview, 2000.

————. *The Quest for Environmental Justice: Human Rights and the Politics of Pollution.* San Francisco: Sierra Club Books, 2005.

Cole, Luke W., and Sheila R. Foster. *From the Ground Up: Environmental Racism and the Rise of the Environmental Justice Movement.* Critical America Series. New York: New York University Press, 2000.

Karenga, Maulana. *Kwanzaa: A Celebration of Family, Community, and Culture.* Commemorative ed. Los Angeles: University of Sankore Press, 1998.

Molina, Mario, and Luisa Molina. "Megacities and Atmospheric Pollution," *Journal of the Air and Waste Management Association* 54 (June 2004): 644–80, available at http://eaps.mit.edu/megacities/2004criticalreview-1.pdf.

Weaver, Jace, ed. *Defending Mother Earth: Native American Perspectives on Environmental Justice.* Maryknoll, NY: Orbis, 1996.

### Organizations and Web Sites

Environmental Justice Resource Center at Clark Atlanta University. www.ejrc.cau.edu.
EPA Environmental Justice. www.epa.gov/compliance/environmentaljustice.

Urban Environment Class. www.es.ucsb.edu/curriculum_info/es116/116proj/newpage
    .htm.
Environmental Justice and Climate Change Initiative. www.ejcc.org/resources_tech
    .html.
Global Justice and Ecology Project. www.globaljusticeecology.org.
Deep South Center for Environmental Justice. www.xula.edu/dscej.

## NOTES

1. http://www.officialkwanzaawebsite.org/NguzoSaba.html.
2. http://www.goupstate.com/apps/pbcs.dll/article?AID=/20030819/NEWS/30
   8190382&SearchID=73185371250000.
3. U.S. Environmental Protection Agency, Office of Policy, Economics, and Inno-
   vation, *The ReGenesis Partnership: A Case Study.* January 2003.
4. Cory Fleming, "When Environmental Justice Hits the Local Agenda: A Profile
   of Spartanburg and Spartanburg County, South Carolina," June 1, 2004,
   accessed at http://www.knowledgeplex.org/news/37998.html.
5. Harold Mitchell, "Citizens in action: Personal struggle spurred the resolve to
   push for community renewal," *South Carolina Herald-Journal,* 5 October 2003.
6. http://www.officialkwanzaawebsite.org/NguzoSaba.html.
7. Ibid.

# Chapter 7

# Revitalizing Local Communities

*Wylin Dassie*

Given the economic challenges directly or indirectly attributable to globalization, churches are responding to more than merely the spiritual needs of individuals within their local communities. Many church members are facing unemployment and economic vulnerability due to the economic restructuring of local economies, which is often a result of changes within an interdependent global market. Many congregations are heeding the call to social justice by educating themselves on economic globalization and by acting on behalf of the economically marginalized. Some of these congregations have responded to the negative effects of economic globalization by implementing community development strategies in their local communities.

Religious congregations play various roles in local communities. Whether they play the role of moral prophetic voice, cultural critic, or social welfare provider, local congregations always teach and encourage principles and values that influence the way people interpret and live in the world. They are also places where individuals develop and practice the virtue of giving or philanthropy. Wise stewardship and sharing of resources are taught in many ways—as spiritual mandate, moral imperative, spiritual practice, expression of faith, or gratitude to God. Local congregations can also be places where individuals are taught civic engagement and volunteerism. Various studies have shown that individuals who give their time and money to local congregations are more likely to have higher rates of giving and support to other causes and charitable organizations (both secular and faith-based).

There is a long-standing debate regarding the role of religion in public life. This debate continually reemerges with economic, social, and political changes, such as those brought about by the current form of globalization that advocates a larger role for the private sector and civil society. Concomitant to globalization and influenced by it are changes in societal expectations of the role of religious institutions. Many congregations and larger denominational bodies have been reevaluating themselves and their role in public life in light of changes attributable to globalization. For example, some local churches have felt the need to be involved in social service work since economic globalization has negatively affected the quality and location of jobs in local communities and since government support for a social safety net has decreased. Several recent administrations in the United States have even endorsed the role of religious organizations in this realm. Yet globalization has also made it harder for religious organizations, especially individual congregations, to get funding for such work due to increasing numbers of nonprofit groups as well as decreasing funding sources.

It is likely that your congregation is already involved in some sort of outreach or mission work, locally or internationally. Part of the vision of a transformed church is involvement in addressing the problems of economic and social injustice in its own community and the larger world; thus mission work is usually one of the activities of communities of faith. In response to the increasing economic disparity in the United States that is a result of economic globalization, many churches are actively engaged in local community development efforts.

In this chapter I will explore the biblical mandate of concern for the poor and needy and show how several congregations have put this biblical mandate into action by rethinking their role in public life and by responding to growing economic disparity. These examples are instructive to other congregations or community groups who are increasingly feeling a disconnect between the world they live in and the healthy and whole world they envision. In addition to examining various strategic responses to economic globalization, I will show how globalization has affected the funding for local communities' development efforts, making it that much harder to generate successful local responses to global realities.

The Gospel of Mark records the story of Jesus having dinner at Simon the leper's home when a woman comes in with an alabaster jar of expensive perfume and anoints him. As the guests frown upon and begin to reprimand her for what they consider wasteful behavior, Jesus comes to her defense with the statement: "For you always have the poor with you" (Mark 14:7). Despite their misuse, these words were not meant to excuse Christians from working for social and economic transformation within their communities and world.

These words come directly from Jesus' rich Judaic tradition. At the core of this tradition, as recorded in the Hebrew Scriptures, is God's concern for the poor and needy. One of the main causes of poverty in early Judaic history was the oppression and exploitation by a power structure that perpetuated inequitable economic and social conditions within society. Recorded in Deuteronomic law is God's mandate regarding the poor: "Since there will never cease to be some in need on the earth, I therefore command you, 'Open your hand to the poor and needy neighbor in your land'" (Deuteronomy 15:11). Jesus echoes this Deuteronomic mandate to care for the poor and needy not just in words but also in deeds. He exemplified what it meant to be openhanded toward the needy; however, his openhandedness went beyond simple charity to transformative social action in partnership with and on behalf of the poor. The poor and needy, those who are economically vulnerable and socially marginalized, are the individuals the church is called to be in partnership with and to serve as Christ did.

## COMMUNITY ECONOMIC DEVELOPMENT

Currently, many find themselves economically vulnerable and marginalized in communities around the globe. Several countries around the world have experienced economic and social destabilization resulting from the processes of globalization. Specifically within urban and rural communities throughout the United States, we have witnessed job loss as changes have occurred in a national labor market that is subject to the vicissitudes of economic globalization. The increased complexity and volatility of local economies due to globalization have left many communities here and abroad spinning from economic restructuring and instability. As jobs and economic opportunities move out of local U.S. communities, residents are rendered vulnerable because they lack educational and professional skills to make mobility a realistic possibility.

### Direct Local Action

As congregations begin to educate themselves about the phenomenon of economic globalization, they quickly realize that the social, economic, and political challenges it directly or indirectly poses to local communities can seem overwhelming. Therefore, many congregations wisely decide to begin addressing the problems attributable to economic globalization within their own backyard. Congregations like Templo Calvario in Santa Ana, California, have implemented community development strategies in response to economic restructuring of local economies.

Templo Calvario has a nonprofit employment program for members of their local community. Like many socially active congregations, they have realized that community members who perceive a church as being concerned about their material needs (food, clothes, shelter, employment, and financial, for instance) will be more open to their spiritual counsel. Templo Calvario's Center for Employment Opportunities is open to individuals within the community regardless of their faith or church membership. It offers career counseling, listings of prospective employers, and assistance with cover letters, resumes, and the interview process. The center also offers assistance with transportation and food if clients are experiencing economic hardship.[1] This program is just one example of the ways congregations are responding to needs of economically vulnerable and marginalized persons within their local communities.

## Making Global Connections

In light of the emergence of transnational grassroots advocacy networks whose efforts have been facilitated by advances in information technology and greater ease in communication and mobility, local communities are in a better position to "think locally and act globally." Development specialist John Clark uses this reversal of the familiar phrase (think globally and act locally) to emphasize the form that local development efforts should take. This requires relating local community development work to global policies and concerns. A small congregation in Texas is modeling how to "think locally and act globally." When their members experienced significant job losses due to plant closings, they connected with the workers' movement in Mexico. In particular they developed a relationship with a small local congregation in the area where the corporation from their community had moved its plant. The corporation eventually closed its Mexico plant in search of even cheaper labor. The workers in both congregations participated in dialogue and mobilized individuals in their respective communities for local and global social action. The congregation in Texas first had to engage in education about workers' rights, grassroots mobilization, and the International Labor Movement. This was done with the assistance of organizations, such as the Highlander Center, that empower grassroots leaders with necessary skills and knowledge in building broad-based movements for change.

Another congregation that is thinking locally and acting globally is Ousley United Methodist Church in Lithonia, Georgia. One of Ousley's particular concerns is with health issues that face their local community and communities abroad, specifically the HIV/AIDS epidemic. They have partnered with Medical Assistance Program (MAP) International, a global health organization that seeks to promote the total health of communities through the provision of essential medicines, prevention and eradication of disease, and promotion of community health development.

In Africa much of MAP's work is focused on HIV/AIDS education, prevention, and care. Ousley's outreach ministry sent a mission team to Kenya to learn about the strategies that local congregations in Africa employed for education, prevention, and care of persons living with HIV/AIDS. Ousley's developing partnership with MAP allows them to learn successful educational and prevention strategies used by faith communities in Africa that they can then adapt for use in their own community. The Ousley congregation understands the importance of learning from those who are already successfully addressing the same issue, albeit in a different context. Through this developing partnership with MAP, the Ousley and Kenyan congregations are able to learn from one another and share their best practices. For example, Ousley learned about an effective training curriculum for compassionately responding to the needs of families and communities adversely affected by the HIV/AIDS epidemic. Based on models in Kenya, they also plan to implement an HIV/AIDS training for leaders and members of the church and community, possibly offering the training in local theological institutions as well. Connecting with congregations in Africa and becoming aware of the actual proportion of this global epidemic opened up what had previously been a taboo topic in their own community. The Ousley church is an example that shows the importance of learning from communities in other parts of the world who face similar challenges and then acting at the local level.

## Broader Economic Development

Some congregations have broadened their reach and developed Community Development Corporations (CDCs).[2] Zion Hill Baptist Church in Atlanta, like many congregations, started out doing community outreach through various mission projects of the church, such as a ministry outreach program at a local nursing home and a local soup kitchen at a homeless shelter. Wanting to have a greater impact on empowering the community, they decided to streamline the disparate mission activities and put them under one umbrella by creating a CDC. The process Zion Hill followed in developing a CDC is instructive for other congregations. It included three main steps: (1) assessment of community needs; (2) establishment of a mission and objectives; and (3) assessment of congregational resources and possible funding sources. Establishing a CDC provided a more focused and coordinated effort and allowed Zion Hill greater flexibility and ability to apply for funds—government and private foundation grants—that would not be available to religious institutions. Most corporate and private donor organizations do not fund churches directly, but will fund an autonomous CDC that is affiliated with a local congregation.

The phenomenon of churches establishing CDCs in order to do mission work in their local community is not new and has been growing steadily over the past several decades. The importance of keeping the needs of those in the community at the forefront and structuring a program to address specific needs is paramount. Unfortunately, many faith-based organizations face the temptation of shaping a program to match the available governmental and institutional funding instead of creating or securing the funds to match the programs that meet the needs of the people.

Zion Hill began with what the people felt their actual needs were in the community. A committee appointed by the pastor made an assessment of the real needs of the community before moving forward with their plans of establishing a CDC. They researched statistics in the Atlanta area regarding homelessness, the HIV/AIDS epidemic, mental illness, housing, poverty, and other crises facing the community. They also talked to individuals within the community who were involved with the prison system, homeless shelters, and various government agencies that attend to the welfare of persons within the local community. The committee had to determine the shape their program would take, the services to provide, the best way to provide them, and who would be the recipients of these services. From their research and needs assessment, the committee determined there was a need for programs to help homeless women and children. They found that there were shelters and programs to address immediate needs of this vulnerable population, but there were no programs that followed homeless women and children all the way through to wholeness, serving their long-term needs.

Once community needs were ascertained, the committee established the mission and objectives of the Zion Hill CDC Outreach Center for homeless women and children. The mission of the center is "[g]uided by the principles of divine love and service, to provide a safe and supportive environment for women and children experiencing homelessness. To encourage spiritual growth, responsible decision making and economic independence."[3] The CDC provides a comprehensive array of services, such as assistance with General Education Development (GED high school equivalency diploma) preparation, literacy enhancement, resume preparation, computer literacy, career counseling, information and referrals for affordable housing, preparation for homeownership, and spiritual counseling. The objectives of the center are "to improve the spiritual and economic well-being of the Atlanta-East Point Community; to provide community revitalization through faith-based initiatives and supportive services for women and their children who are experiencing homelessness."[4]

The next step that Zion Hill took in establishing their CDC was assessment of their congregation's human and financial resources. Faith-based organizations that do outreach work within their community usually rely heavily upon volunteer services and donations from individuals. Congregations such as Zion Hill can also look to private foundation and corporate funds as well as public funds. Local congregations, the majority of which are small, have less access to government funding, however, as it generally goes to larger organizations. Thus, small nonprofit organizations and religious institutions depend mainly on philanthropy—private contributions of both time and money—to operate.

Zion Hill's outreach center relies heavily on volunteer and in-kind services to meet the needs of the women and children they serve. Instead of relying on outside funding, the congregation agreed to make the commitment to support the center's work financially for the initial phase of operation. However, they have not ruled out the possibility of seeking outside funding from government or private foundation sources. Knowing the advantages and disadvantages of such support is important. For instance, government funding comes with strict stipulations about how and when issues of faith can be communicated in an effort to prevent government-funded proselytizing.

Of the three main sectors that make up the American economy (business, government, and nonprofit), the nonprofit sector is the second largest in terms of numbers. It comprises over one million organizations and provides a significant share of goods and services that are consumed by the American population.[5] Total private giving to the nonprofit sector doubled within the past decade, reaching about $178 billion in 1998 and nearly $200 billion by the twenty-first century.[6] Gifts from individuals (including bequests) have historically constituted 85 to 90 percent of all private giving.[7]

Religious communities and organizations are a fundamental segment of the nonprofit sector and historically have received the largest share of total private giving among the nine subsectors (between 43 to 53 percent during the past two decades).[8] In absolute terms, private contributions have been consistent over the past several decades, but there has been increased competition for funding from other nonprofit organizations, such as international relief agencies, international economic development organizations, and policy research and advocacy organizations that rely heavily on private funds. With heightened awareness of the interconnectedness of local and global issues, the formation of networks and associations with nongovernmental organizations (NGOs) around the world and in the nonprofit sector here in the United States has increased. This formation of networks has facilitated the ability of these international grassroots organizations to solicit American donors for funds. In addition, from 1987 through 1997 U.S. nonprofits have grown by 30 percent while public funding for such ventures has dwindled.[9] In a situation of scarcity, local congregations find it hard to compete with large nonprofits that can do bigger development projects. Furthermore, not all donors fund religious institutions.

## CONCLUSIONS

As a congregation or community group gets more involved in transforming a community through local community development efforts or as one contemplates how to strengthen existing efforts, a clear strategy and focus are essential. Zion Hill provides a helpful example of the initial steps involved in the decision to be a more effective transformative force within a community.

Streamlining their mission work by developing a CDC was the first step. The second step was the establishment of solid partnerships with existing community organizations such as other nonprofit organizations or local governmental agencies that are already addressing the needs of the target population. For example, among their various partnerships with other nonprofit or governmental organizations, Zion Hill worked with Atlanta Union Mission, which helped them secure affordable housing for some of the women and children they serve.

Establishing a CDC is not an appropriate strategy for all congregations or community groups. Some congregations can meet local community needs by simply partnering with existing local nonprofit or governmental organizations that are already offering services that complement and enhance the impact of the church's mission work. Establishing strong partnerships with other organizations is also a way to lessen the impact of globalization on funding at the local level. For example, through various partnerships, Zion Hill is able to reduce its operational costs and offer services free of charge that they, by themselves, do not have the capacity to provide.

Although Zion Hill has a comprehensive program, some congregations have the capacity or desire to be involved only in smaller community development projects. Some congregations partner with local educators and volunteers in the community to offer computer literacy classes and other essential job training skills for people in their communities. Others offer GED tutorials. Still others foster economic development by providing unused space (e.g., a spare room) for fledgling and resource-poor entrepreneurs to access such amenities as fax and copy machines and computers with useful business management or desktop publishing software.

Congregations who are interested in addressing the problems associated with economic globalization must first decide what services they want to provide to their community, whether direct services, advocacy, or education. Providing direct services can include meeting the immediate needs of individuals in the community as Zion Hill did or offering professional training as Templo Calvario did. Advocacy and education are often overlooked or given less credibility by congregations, yet we should not disregard the power congregations have to advocate for underserved or neglected populations who are rendered silent by their lack of political or economic power. Advocacy can include writing letters or visiting local political officials who make decisions that will affect the lives of underserved people within a community. Congregations can also raise awareness on numerous issues connected to economic globalization, as the Ousley congregation did in promoting dialogue about HIV/AIDS and as the Texas congregation did in addressing corporate accountability. These educational campaigns motivated congregational members to increase their financial support and involvement in addressing the needs wrought by economic globalization.

After deciding what services to provide, congregations must develop a plan for implementing their outreach ministry. They can establish a CDC as Zion Hill did or partner with other groups, such as local congregations, governmental or private organizations, or global networks of churches and faith-based organizations that address particular issues. Congregations have a salient role to play in local community development, especially with unmet needs increasing in the global economy. The point to remember is that no one strategy fits all communities, for each community has unique needs and strengths.

## QUESTIONS FOR DISCUSSION

1. What mission projects is your congregation currently involved with? How can you work to get more of your members involved with these projects?
2. Can you envision doing an assessment of the needs of your community? How might you go about it? What do you think you might find? Is your congregation ready to take on a new ministry project that responds to local community needs? What preparations might you need to undertake in order to get your congregation to that point?
3. Dassie claims that Christians should be involved in community development because of God's concern for the poor and needy. How do the Bible and the example of Jesus help us think about our community responsibilities? Can you think of other biblical themes or stories that motivate you to be involved?

## RESOURCES

### Books and Articles

Klein, Kim. *Fundraising in Times of Crisis*. San Francisco: Jossey-Bass, 2004.

Kretzmann, John P., and John L. McKnight. *Building Communities from the Inside Out: A Path Toward Finding and Mobilizing a Community's Assets*. Chicago: ACTA, 1993.

Prokosch, Mike, and Laura Raymond. *The Global Activist's Manual: Local Ways to Change the World*. New York: Nation Books, 2002.

Robinson, Andy. *Grassroots Grants: An Activist's Guide to Grantseeking*. 2nd ed. San Francisco: Jossey-Bass, 2004.

Sen, Rinku. *Stir It Up: Lessons in Community Organizing and Advocacy*. San Francisco: Jossey-Bass, 2003.

Weitzman, Murray S., Nadine T. Jalandoni, Linda M. Lampkin, and Thomas Pollak. *The New Nonprofit Almanac and Desk Reference*. San Francisco: Jossey-Bass, 2002.

### Organizations and Web Sites

The Foundation Center. www.fdncenter.org.

Highlander Center. www.highlandercenter.org.

Grass-Roots. www.grass-roots.org.

Christian Community Development Association. www.ccda.org.
National Congress for Community Economic Development. www.ncced.org.
Center for Faith-Based and Community Initiatives. www.hhs.gov/fbci.

## NOTES

1. Christian Reformed World Relief Committee, Development Stories. "Church Offers Employment Help," May 6, 2005. http://www.crwrc.org/?action=d7_ article_display&Join_ID=86101.
2. A CDC is a grassroots organization, usually formed and controlled by community stakeholders such as residents, clergy, service providers, or business proprietors. CDCs usually serve a neighborhood or cluster of neighborhoods, and are typically organized as nonprofit 501(c) 3 corporations whose mission is the revitalization of poor communities. See Avis C. Vidal, "CDCs as Agents of Neighborhood Change: The State of the Art," in *Revitalizing Urban Neighborhoods,* ed. W. Dennis Keating et al. (Lawrence, KS: University Press of Kansas, 1996), 149–63.
3. Zion Hill Community Development Corporation brochure.
4. Ibid.
5. Murray S. Weitzman et al., *The New Nonprofit Almanac and Desk Reference* (San Francisco: Jossey-Bass, 2002), 3–7.
6. Ibid., 52.
7. Ibid.
8. The nine subsectors of the nonprofit sector are Religion, Education, Health, Human Services, Arts, Public and Societal Benefit, Environment, International and Foreign Affairs, and Unclassified Organizations (Weitzman et al., *Almanac*), xxvi, 56.
9. Ibid., 9.

# Chapter 8

# Creating the Commons

*Larry Rasmussen*

We are "born to belonging."[1] "Biological-social" is the kind of creature we are. When others first heard our borning cry, we could not walk, feed ourselves, don clothing, or provide elemental protection—not from the heat, the cold, starvation, or those who might do us harm. For a long while, only the care of others would keep us alive, just as only the mentoring of others would teach us basic life skills. Even as adults we could not make a No. 2 yellow lead pencil on our own, or provide the nutrients for a healthy meal from scratch. We stand on the shoulders of ancestors, compatriots, and anonymous millions. Our own journey begins with their legacy. Not least, when dying day comes and we return to the topsoil we are, we will join in yet another way the great community of life that birthed us. We are born to belonging, and we die into it.

This is true for us not only as biological-social individuals but also as card-carrying members of a rambunctious, even aggressive, species. If anything, the communion with all life deepens from this vantage point. When David Hillis and his colleagues at the University of Texas tried to display the relationship of three thousand species of animals, plants, fungi, and microbes (out of 10 to 100 million species!), they decided that what served their scientific purpose best was an ancient religious symbol Darwin himself chose for his blockbuster work, *On the Origins of Species*. "The affinities of all the beings of the same class have sometimes been represented as a great tree," Darwin wrote in his concluding pages. "I believe this simile largely speaks the truth. The green and budding twigs may represent existing species; and those produced during each former year may represent the long succession of extinct species. . . . As buds give rise by growth to fresh buds, and these, if vigorous, branch out and overtop on all sides many a feebler branch, so by generation I believe it has been with the great Tree of Life, which fills with its dead and broken branches the crust of the earth, and covers the surface with its ever branching and beautiful ramifications."[2] Hillis and colleagues shaped their tree of life a bit oddly, more like a bicycle wheel than a tree, with each species represented as the tip of a spoke-like branch ending along the rim. Even with this helpful graphic the tree became so dense they needed an additional aid for anyone trying to find *Homo sapiens sapiens*. So a big arrow announces "You are here" and points to our dot along the rim. From there the eye travels back down the branch that joins us to chimpanzees, our closest living relatives, onto the larger branch of our common ancestor, next to all vertebrates, then all animals, and finally into the largest and deepest branches meeting at the center of the tree. This is the home, in the heartwood, of the common ancestors of all living things. That is where we are, finally, and what we are, in the end. We are belongers to a fierce communion that Mendel's progeny, supplementing Darwin's, now track in the DNA sap rising everywhere in the tree.[3] The Earth Charter puts it simply: "Humanity is part of a vast evolving universe. Earth, our home, is alive with a unique community of life."[4]

But where does Earth belong? Was it also "born to belonging"? Here science, itself no stranger to metaphor and imagination, shares turf with religion. Most religions have not only claimed from time immemorial that the human is a microcosm of the macrocosm, an embodiment, even a mirror, of the universe itself. They surpass that with another claim: creation, all of it, is best understood in terms of community, a cosmic community. Science may not readily embrace that language per se, but its message often comes surprisingly close. Recall those first posters of galaxies. Some showed great pillars of gaseous clouds: one is titled "Pillars of Creation." Others offered a panoply of galaxy lights spread across the black reaches of space. One of these has our familiar arrow, "You are here." This time it does not point to a branch in the tree of life, however, but to a smudge in the Milky Way. It points to Earth, our home. Each of us is not only a small branch of the tangled tree of life. Each is far older, a late galactic version of stardust and gasses originating in the big bang. We belong among the stars, together with the rest of the tree of life and the rest of our solar system. We are at home in the cosmos and the cosmos is at home in us. Plato was not wholly wrong, then, in thinking that the souls inhabiting our bodies come from the stars. So does Earth's body, and the galaxy bodies as well, with all their stars and planets. Creation, all of it, together, is a vast community, a "uni-verse" of infinite makeup.[5]

As we turn to Christian ethics and the subject of land, the commons, and the environment, this is the grand canvas on which we begin: with creation as the most fundamental dimension of every other community that ever was or ever will be. We are not human apart from our home here and have never been human anywhere else.

Nor, for that matter, are we truly human apart from a sense of wonder and mystery over it all. Augustine's words about "the standing miracle" of earth and sky are apt: "Although . . . the standing miracle of this visible world is little thought of, because always before us, yet, when we arouse ourselves to contemplate it, it is a greater miracle than the rarest and most unheard-of marvels."[6]

Unless we begin with creation as community and the "standing miracle" of life, our appraisal of land, the commons, and the environment easily falls to the besetting sin of most moderns: a nonrelational consciousness toward most of the universe, together with an utterly instrumental use of life as little more than a stack of "resources." Despite growing knowledge of both the evolution of the universe and the evolution of earth's tree of life, modern consciousness frequently spins a cocoon of isolated subjectivity, a subjectivity with little feeling for nonhuman members of the community of life and little feeling for the exploding stars from which all is born. Those feelings dead and gone, we lose our sense of belonging, together with a sense for our stark dependence and indebtedness. Not least we lose our sense of belonging to the land as bone of our bone and flesh of our flesh, just as we lose sight of land and environment as the commons we share and the indispensable condition of every life.

Take that No. 2 yellow pencil mentioned above. Try making one on your own, from scratch. Where will you get the tin for the crinkled band? How will you know which ore to search for and how will you know where to find it? How will you mine and process it until pliant enough for the thin little circle that holds eraser and stem together? Where will you get the rubber for the eraser? Who will suggest the unlikely place of a tree's innards? How will you know which tree, and then find it? When you do, what will you do to get an eraser from the sticky, whitish fluid someone told you to tap? What about the other materials—the graphite, for instance? Where do you find that? What is it, anyway? (It's not lead.) What makes it write? If it does not write by itself, how do you get it to do so? Then there is the pencil stem. What material is best for that? Plastic or wood? If plastic, what is it made from, since there is no such thing as plastic ore or living plastic plants? And how do you get from its mysterious material source to a working pencil shape? If wood, how will you harvest, saw, and finish it in the hexagonal or circular shape of a pencil? Lastly, don't forget to paint it. With what? What is paint, anyway? For that matter, what is color? And how do you get the thick liquid just the right shade so that the No. 2 pencil is yellow and not amber or chartreuse?

This pencil is obviously not a task for you by yourself. It is the work of thousands, perhaps tens of thousands, over centuries. Some very complex systems of local and global knowledge, invention, mechanics, trade, and commerce are in play.

Still, all this human activity comes rather late in the game. If No. 2 pencils were the product of human genius, spirit, ideas, and cooperation only, we would still have nothing, nada, zip. Where did the tin ore come from? How was it formed over eons? How did it get where it is? What about the tree for wood or the petroleum products for plastics? When and how did they evolve? From what? If you were assigned to create a tree, what chemicals would you gather? And how would you fix the mix to arrive at life in this specific botanical form? The same holds for the rubber, the graphite, and color. What, where, how come? By what nigh-eternal forces and processes? For your pencil, then, you can thank the standing miracle of land, air, water, sunlight, and endless minute and enormous transactions age in and age out. In fact, you can literally thank your lucky stars. Both you and your No. 2 pencil were born to belonging long, long ago.

From its inception, Christian ethics has argued that creation is a commons to which we belong. And it has argued that the commons makes moral claims upon us as trustees, stewards, or, for that matter, simply fellow creatures in the shared cosmos of interdependent life.

These moral claims are often forgotten, especially when we treat the life of the commons in the nonrelational, utilitarian terms of commodities for human markets. Nature's gifts as goods and services are, of course, utterly necessary for life itself. Every species is utterly nature-indebted. Certainly biological-social creatures like us cannot live otherwise. As adult humans we are no less radically dependent upon the rest of nature than we were as newborns. Still, we easily forget our belonging to one another and the commons; and we forget the moral claims that issue from shared existence.

Fortunately, someone usually speaks up against the forgetting and against abuse. They may speak up in the manner of Ambrose in the fourth century:

> Why do the injuries of nature delight you? The world has been created for all, while you rich are trying to keep it for yourselves. Not merely the possession of the earth, but the very sky, air and the sea are claimed for the use of the rich few. . . . Not from your own do you bestow on the poor man, but you make return from what is his. For what has been given as common for the use of all, you appropriate for yourself alone. The earth belongs to all, not to the rich.[7]

Or they may speak up in the manner of Wendell Berry in the twentieth century, bewailing the complicity of Christianity itself in ravaging the commons.

> [Modern Christianity] has, for the most part, stood silently by while a predatory economy has ravaged the world, destroyed its natural beauty

and health, divided and plundered its human communities and house-holds. It has flown the flag and chanted the slogans of empire. It has assumed with the economists that "economic factors" automatically work for good and has assumed with the industrialists and militarists that tech-nology determines history. It has assumed with almost everybody that "progress" is good, that it is good to be modern and with the times. It has admired Caesar and comforted him in his depredations and defaults. But in its de facto alliance with Caesar, Christianity connives in the murder of Creation. But in these days, Caesar is no longer a mere destroyer of armies, cities, and nations. He is a contradictor of the fundamental miracle of life.[8]

But people do not only speak up. Some, like Berry, also live in ways that sim-ply assume they are born to belonging and that creation is the commons whose physical and moral reality rightly binds them. For them religion, morality, and ecology are all about much the same thing: bonds that connect the world and hold it together. Religion, morality, and ecology, as woven into daily habits, are about relationships and responsibilities that tether us to other beings and other forces. If we want no conniving part "in the murder of Creation," we might turn, then, to these exemplars, however modest, and learn from them. They take the commons seriously in an era when economic globalization does not take it seriously, despite utter dependence upon it.

Five examples follow. Two are very small scale, humble in size and influence. A third is an agricultural movement across several lands, though local and regional in the way it works. A fourth adds business and industry to agriculture and models regional integration. All four of these are self-conscious, "insider" responses to the destructive side of economic globalization and its industrial-ization of agriculture. The fifth is different. It is the survival effort of those suf-ficiently marginalized by the first wave of globalization so as to be left almost wholly outside the workings of the global economy today. Yet all these exam-ples, different as they are, share a vital trait. They honor the land and the local community as the commons. Most, though not all, are explicitly Christian in their honed sense for creation and its moral claims.

The Community Farm Project of Santa Fe, New Mexico, announces itself with a psalm of gratitude and indebtedness. The first page of its green infor-mation flyer reads: "The eyes of all look to you, and you give them their food in due season. You open your hand, satisfying the desire of every living thing" (Psalm 145:15–16). The Community Farm is privately owned by John Stephenson, but in 1984 he began working with New Vistas, an organization serving developmentally disabled persons in Santa Fe. Stephenson wanted them to learn about farming, enjoy its bonds with the land, and enjoy their own part in the land's yield. The collaborative project grew, as did the crops, and soon Stephenson and New Vistas began delivering fruit and vegetables to the hun-gry of Santa Fe, working through a dozen agencies from shelters to food pantries to soup kitchens to youth centers and senior centers. The forty acres outstripped what Stephenson and New Vista volunteers could handle and soon members of the First Presbyterian Church of Santa Fe and the Ghost Ranch in Santa Fe Education and Retreat Center established a volunteer program to join the farm-work. That has since expanded to include the Boy Scouts and Girl Scouts, Elderhostel, Intermountain Youth Center, La Casita School, Montessori School, St. John's College, St. John's United Methodist Church, and the Santa Fe Public Schools. These members of the Community Farm plant, weed, prune, harvest, clean, and deliver what normally totals about $200,000 worth of fruit and vegetables annually for local needs. Because the U.S. Southwest continues in a drought, they have learned to do this with an irrigation system that uses less water than most local farming. Community Farm members learn to know the soil and honor its needs at the same time they and the land serve basic community health and nutrition needs. This not only expresses the Community Farm's psalm of gratitude to God. It recalls a theme of the Hebrew Bible that the desert, too, yields abundantly when the people act wisely and justly.

The urban version of the Community Farm has sprung up in many large cities in recent decades, in the form of community gardens. These are not truly farms, even though many grow produce together with flowers. Most reclaim city "brownfields," sites not toxic enough to qualify for government cleanup treatment, but despoiled enough not to be used. Many are the strewed remains of a city lot where once a building stood. Neighbors claim the site as a community commons and restore the land to cultivation, sometimes taking it back from drug dealers or gangs. More often than not, a neighborhood mural soon graces a wall on one side or another of the greening "brownfield" and a gazebo for music making or benches and small tables for checkers, chess, or simply conversation and a bite to eat appear. Young and old occupy the space, either for work or leisure or both. Sometimes a small corner becomes a play area for preschool children whose parents are working in the garden. Whatever the particular features are, the testimony is invariably the same: the pleasure of growing the food and flowers is real, but the way this reclaimed land has brought the neighborhood together as community in a harsh setting is the real joy. (At last count, New York City, to cite but one case, had more than seven hundred community gardens.)

The third example is much like the first except that it has become a large network that produces for local markets rather than for local charities. Community Supported Agriculture (CSA) is a conscious reaction against the industrialization of agriculture in the hands of corporations and other large landholders. CSA is about farming as a way of life rather than an industry or even a livelihood (in the form of wages and profits). Ties to the land and its requirements for regeneration on its own intrinsic terms are fundamental, and all CSA farms are "organic"—no manufactured herbicides or pesticides are used. Some CSA farms are also "biodynamic"—the farm itself produces all the elements needed to sustain itself as a complete biosystem. (Animals are critical for this, thus pushing these CSA farms beyond organic gardening only.) But whether organic, biodynamic, or both, the ties of CSA farmers to the land extend beyond the farm. There is a conscious and necessary connection of rural to urban by which urban dwellers "subscribe" to the farm. Urban partners provide the farmer needed cash flow, via annual subscriptions, in exchange for weekly delivery of fresh organic produce during the harvesting season. (Harvests typically run many months, often a half year, with early crops like greens; middle-season crops like sweet corn, carrots, onions, and berries; and late crops like apples, pears, squash, and potatoes.) Many members of CSA farms also spend time on "their" farm as volunteers. They frequently exchange recipes as well and organize potlucks now and again at the place of their weekly pickup (churches often serve as pickup sites). In a word, community is fostered around good and healthy food and around a rural-urban link in which urban CSA members take some of the risks the farmer does (some years are markedly better than others, some crops are better than others, and disasters such as drought or hail can happen). This remains market-oriented agriculture but the market is local, personal, and direct. It is a way of life that is also a living for the farmer. And it is genuinely *community-supported* agriculture: the recipients of the fresh produce are members of the community that enjoys the yield of the land even as they help it produce "its fruit in due season" (Psalm 145:15). North America, parts of South America, Asia, and Europe, together with Australia and New Zealand, all have active CSA communities.

The fourth example is explicitly Christian in origin and conception, though it has become interfaith in recent years. The Focolare Movement started as a group of women in Trent, Italy, amid the destruction of World War II and around the leadership of twenty-three-year-old Chiara Lubich. *Focolare* is Italian for "hearth" or "family fireplace" and was chosen as a symbol pointing to the reconstruction of life by a small group around an intimate central energy point in the experience of the love of God. Roman Catholic in origin and committed to living all of life in the light of the gospel, the movement now has several million followers in over 180 countries. Of interest here is a global economic project begun in 1991 by Focolare members in Brazil: the "Economy of Communion." The heart of this now dispersed but worldwide economy is business and finance dedicated to radical, or gospel, values in the workplace with a view to a socially just and environmentally sustainable economic order. The original inspiration is clearly Roman Catholic sacramentalism with a strong sense of the Mystical Body of Christ. Yet many Focolare members are not Catholic and some are not Christian. Nonetheless, common principles and a shared sacramental spirituality permeate the Economy of Communion.

Broadly speaking, the Economy of Communion pursues the possibility of reforming global capitalism in socially and environmentally sustainable directions congruent with "gospel values." That is, enterprises operate within the free market, use numerous common business practices, and abide by business regulations. But they also divide all profits three ways: one-third to the poor, one-third for business reinvestment, and one-third for the formation of people in Focolare spirituality. As of 2003, there were 693 small- and medium-size businesses in the Economy of Communion network, in Europe, Latin America, North America, Asia, Australia, and Africa; 194 were engaged in production, 156 in commerce, and 343 in services. Only ten have more than one hundred employees.

The Economy of Communion is reformist in that it lives by communitarian values within an economic order dominated by instrumental values. The effort is to bring religious-moral substance into the workplace as a community place, within a capitalist framework. Distinctive emphases toward this end follow, all of them a conscious outgrowth of Focolare spirituality. *Work* is viewed as cocreating with God. It offers both personal fulfillment and a means of community service. *Trade, finance, and industry* are oriented to communitarian ends, such as alleviating poverty and spreading the wealth. Debt is strongly discouraged, although low-interest microfinancing and other alternative financing structures have been developed in recent years. Trade, finance, and industry are not meant, in any event, to promote or bolster a consumer lifestyle. They are means to help create communities of material sufficiency and equality. *Wealth and possessions* are put at the disposal of the common good. Focolare members are encouraged in simple living, voluntarily offering any surplus resources to the communion of goods. Tithing is expected. A strong trust in providence ("God will provide!") has been a theme since the beginnings in the 1940s. *Economic exchange* is viewed as a meeting of moral agents or "ethical actors." The market is appreciated and used for its efficiency, but the social function of every economic encounter is communion; that is, the rationale for economic exchange is building up human community in face-to-face exchange of persons who take responsibility for themselves and others. *Protection of the environment* is part of economic activity itself, and is the object of both personal responsibility and corporate policy. Economy and environment are not conceptualized separately; they belong together and together they belong to the commons. *Technological progress* is viewed positively when it expresses creativity directed to community well-being. The health of the community assumes a healthy economy and environment; both can be enhanced with sophisticated scientific knowledge and appropriate technology.[9]

If the Focolare Movement's Economy of Communion is a workplace reform effort within the largely urbanized framework of global capitalism, our last example is one of subsistence agriculture and village life several steps removed from such a framework. It is largely untouched by the daily workings of economic globalization. It is thus largely independent of both the benefits and burdens of globalization. At the same time, this organization's very reason for existence rests in the drastic consequences of the initial wave of globalization. That first wave was the colonization of lands around the world by European powers beginning in the fifteenth century and the establishment of neo-European civilization on every continent except Antarctica. This was the first time the economy went truly "global." It was the onset of planetary economic integration on European and neo-European terms.

This is the backdrop for the African Association of Earthkeeping Churches (AAEC), made up of about two million Shona Christians in southern Zimbabwe. Their slogan is "Regaining the Lost Lands, Reclothing the Earth." The lands were lost three times in three ways. The first was the initial wave of economic colonization and globalization just mentioned. In this case, English settlers following Cecil Rhodes took the most fertile lands from the Shona in the process of establishing "Rhodesia" as a neo-European settler nation. Next, the promised agricultural reform that was a goal of the 1970s/1980s War of Independence by the "Sons of the Soil," as the rebels called themselves, failed to take place. The colonized lands were not regained, at least locally, even though colonial Rhodesia became independent Zimbabwe. Finally, the lands were lost to deforestation and erosion as impoverished Shona peoples tried to eke out a living from the hard-scrabble granite hills to which they had been forcefully removed.

"Reclothing the Earth" is the name these same farmers give their efforts to reforest their lands, to save its soil and bring it back to full health, and to harvest rainwater and stream water. Villages of the AAEC now have their own nurseries, in keeping with community decisions about desired species for future purposes, and young people are trained in local horticulture and land preservation. The "reclothing" itself is enacted liturgically. Christian rites attend planting, harvesting, feasting, and saving seed. Many are Shona Christian adaptations of Hebrew Bible festivals, such as the Feast of Booths. The theology is thoroughly Christocentric, however. Colossians 1:17 is the verse on the AAEC logo, which pictures an African farmer planting a tree: "In Christ all things hold together." Jesus Christ is Earthkeeper and Healer of the Land.

Yet AAEC work is interfaith as well as Christian. Practitioners of traditional, or indigenous, Shona religion are organized as the Association of Zimbabwean Traditional Ecologists (AZTREC). They join Shona Christians of the AAEC in joint labors and participate appropriately in one another's rituals. Their labors include sponsorship together of the Zimbabwean Institute of Religious Research and Ecological Conservation (ZIRRCON). All this is work done by people rooted in a place, albeit after having been uprooted from neighboring places. They assume the local commons as their life arena and seek to restore its health as intrinsic to their own.

These five examples, while disparate, can be viewed as different elements of a sophisticated strategy. Responding constructively to the destructive downside of corporate economic globalization requires a wide range of diverse efforts. Some will be reformist, working within the capitalist framework but bending that framework in communitarian ways at every point possible and giving it a spirituality it does not carry in its own utilitarian soul. Both the Focolare Movement and Community Supported Agriculture do this, in ways appropriate to both agriculture and commerce. Some will be, on the face of it, intentionally local with no aim in view to create regional or global networks. They nonetheless build up community and meet local community needs by means of in-place institutions under their control. Little is required beyond hands-on education, volunteer coordination, and active networking by agencies already in existence. The Community Farm Project and its exercise in learning to love the land in the process of putting it to community use is such an effort. So is the community gardens movement in large cities. Still another strategy for saving and nurturing the commons that saves and nurtures us sits at the far edge of globalization dynamics. Its very alienation is ironically its advantage, since the community depends almost wholly upon its own resources. The resulting communal independence, harsh though it may be, offers an opportunity to create sustainable community on terms other than those allowed and constrained by corporate economic globalization. The AAEC occupies this terrain.

In short, the commons and its communities are the shared elements of an implicit strategy, a strategy that works both inside and at the edges of the global economy. It is reformist and radical in varying degrees, and it is varied in scale and reach, from a single community to networks across regions and countries, even continents. Yet its common object of steady attention is always the same: healthy local community.

A sophisticated strategy requires other elements as well, and they are not provided here—mass movements and macro-institutions and policies, for example. The point, however, is that we all have something vital to learn from these five examples. They are the work of those who understand belonging. They understand creation as a community and they practice "an economy of communion" that embraces people and the land together, in common.

## QUESTIONS FOR DISCUSSION

1. Rasmussen offers five living examples of how groups have come together to "create the commons." What do you regard as examples of "commons" in your community? How does the existence of common spaces and activities (or the lack thereof) impact the culture and feel of your community? How might your congregation work together toward "creating the commons"?

2. Rasmussen claims that a sense of belonging to the land is a prerequisite for strategies of reclaiming the commons. How can we individually and communally rekindle this sense of belonging to the land?

Why is honoring the land and the local community as the commons important in an increasingly globalizing world?

3. Rasmussen contrasts different value systems—communitarian, utilitarian, instrumental, and gospel values. What are the key values in each of these systems? Which value system(s) do you attempt to follow? Are different value systems appropriate in different spheres of life? (For instance, utilitarianism in the political sphere.) Why or why not?

## RESOURCES

### Books and Articles

Rasmussen, Larry. *Earth Community, Earth Ethics*. Maryknoll, NY: Orbis, 1996.
Snyder, Gary. "The Place, the Region, and the Commons." Pages 471–86 in *Environmental Philosophy: From Animal Rights to Radical Ecology*. Ed. Michael Zimmerman, J. Baird Callicot, George Sessions, Karen J. Warren, and John Clark. 3rd ed. Upper Saddle River, NJ: Prentice-Hall, 2001.
Shiva,Vandana. "Women in the Forest." Pages 55–95 in *Staying Alive: Women, Ecology and Development*. London: Zed, 1989.

### Organizations and Web Sites

American Community Garden Association. www.communitygarden.org.
Community Gardens in New York City. www.greenguerillas.org.
Community Land Trusts. www.iceclt.org/clt.
Community Supported Agriculture (CAS) Farm Directory. www.landstewardshipproj ect.org/csa.html.
Friends of the Commons. www.friendsofthecommons.org.
Network of Earthkeeping Christian Communities in South Africa. www.neccsa.org.za.

## NOTES

1. The title of the book by Mab Segrest: *Born to Belonging: Writings on Spirit and Justice* (New Brunswick, NJ: Rutgers University Press, 2002).
2. As cited by Stephen Jay Gould, "This View of Life," *Natural History* 102, no. 12 (1993): 19.
3. Cited from Carl Zimmer, "You Are Here," a review of Richard Dawkins, *The Ancestor's Tale: A Pilgrimage to the Dawn of Evolution,* in *The New York Times Book Review,* Sunday, 17 October 2004, 30.
4. *The Earth Charter,* Preamble. The text of the charter is available on the Web site of The Earth Charter Secretariat: www.earthcharter.org.
5. It may be coincidental but it is hardly unfitting that the cosmologist who first proposed the big bang as the theory of creation, Georges-Henri Lemaître, was an ordained priest, any more unfitting than that the father of genetics, Thomas Mendel, was a monk, and the paleontologist who placed us amid the epic drama of energy and evolution, Pierre Teilhard de Chardin, was also an ordained

priest. Their religious sense of a sacred cosmos as a community merged with the minutiae of the science that awed them. By such reckoning as theirs, the primary and primordial revelation of God *is* the universe itself, and creation as community is the hymn of the universe.

6. Augustine, *City of God,* Modern Library Classics (NY: Random House, 2000), 10, 12.

7. From *De Nabuthe Jezraelita* 3.11, as cited by Rosemary Radford Ruether, "Sisters of Earth: Religious Women and Ecological Spirituality," *The Witness* 83, no. 5 (May 2000): 14.

8. Wendell Berry, *Sex, Economy, Freedom & Community* (New York: Pantheon, 1993), 115.

9. This information has been gathered from the Web site of the Focolare Movement: www.rc.net/focolare/whatis.htm; and from Lorna Gold, "The Roots of the Focolare Movement's Economic Ethic," in *Journal of Markets & Morality,* 6, no. 1 (2003): 1–14.

# PART THREE
# PUBLIC POLICY STRATEGIES

# Chapter 9

# Promoting Solidarity with Migrants
*Daisy L. Machado*

> *I say the class of immigrants coming to the shores of the United States at this time are not the kind of people we want as citizens of this country.*
> —Representative James V. McClintic (D.-Okla.),
> Congressional Record, Dec. 10, 1921, 177.[1]

The United States is a nation that has played a particular role in world history. Serving as a safe haven for those seeking liberty and self-determination since the seventeenth century, the United States has promoted itself as a nation whose roots are firmly planted in an immigrant past. It is a nation that, except for the Native Peoples, is entirely made up of people who were not born here. Some were brought here forcefully as slaves, many others were immigrants who left their past behind them in order to enter a land perceived as one of promise and new beginnings. Despite the national historical imagination that continues to promote an immigrant past as a badge of honor, however, this nation has, throughout its history, expressed unease about the people who are entering its shores. From the early Puritan conflicts with the Quakers, who were banished from a number of colonies including the colony of New Amsterdam in what is now New York, to the conflicts with Roman Catholics and Jews, to the fear expressed that the immigrants coming to the United States were little more than the "common class of vagrants, paupers and other outcasts of Europe,"[2] a sense of ambivalence has permeated this nation's relations with its immigrant arrivals. While the economic benefits of immigrants to the expanding national

115

economy was prized, nevertheless nativism and the rise of nativist groups increased after 1830 when rapid social and economic change was accompanied by a rise in immigration.

Those who opposed immigration in the first decades of the 1900s argued that the new wave of immigrants were inferior to previous waves and therefore unfit to become American citizens. These fears were corroborated by the findings of the Dillingham Commission established by Congress in 1907. The 42-volume report, the result of four years of investigation, asserted that

> the post-1890 immigrants were economically inferior to the older European types . . . and that the children of immigrants were more apt to be criminals than were children of native-born Americans. . . . At bottom its bias formed the basis of its conclusions that peoples of southern and eastern Europe were inferior to those of northern and western Europe, and hence should be restricted. The ban on Asians should also be maintained said the Commission's majority. The Commissioners' final recommendation was for a literacy test, such as that proposed by the Immigration Restriction League. . . . Now newcomers would have to be literate in order to pass through Ellis Island.[3]

Given the findings of the Dillingham Commission it is not surprising that Congress would develop national origins quotas or that these quotas, which thoroughly reduced immigration from the undesirable nations of southern and eastern Europe, were based on the "expert" advice of eugenicists like Harry Laughlin, who in 1920 became the "eugenics expert" for the House Committee on Immigration and Naturalization.[4]

During World War I, Mexican immigrants helped make up for the shortage of workers created by the war. But the Mexican immigrants were as unwelcome in the 1930s as were Asians and Europeans from southern and eastern Europe. Americans, especially in the Southwest, thought no better of Mexicans than they did of Italians or Russians or Polish Jews. In that wave of immigration the southwestern borderlands developed a distinct culture and reality of life that to this day continues to influence and shape the lives of Tejanos who live north of the Rio Grande and the lives of the borderlands people in Mexico who live south of the Rio Grande. The history of the Texas borderlands provided a distinctive background for how the relations between the white Texans and the Mexicans and Mexican-American Tejanos would develop.

## THE UNITED STATES AND MEXICO BORDERLANDS

Let me begin by defining the idea of borderlands. The well-known historian Herbert Eugene Bolton first used the term "borderlands," or more specifically "Spanish borderlands," in the context of U.S. or North American history. Bolton coined the phrase in 1921 and used it in his presidential address, delivered in 1932, before the American Historical Association. By his idea of borderlands Bolton was proposing to introduce a "broader approach to American history, one that was not simply Anglo-oriented or limited to the study of the thirteen colonies."[5] Bolton was creating a historical space for the writing of a North American history that would be more than an "unhistorical Anglo epic."[6] Bolton argued that American historians could not continue to ignore the nearly three centuries of Spanish presence in the southwestern half of the United States. Borderlands history was, for Bolton, the recognition that the writing of U.S. history had traditionally been done in "isolation, apart from its setting in the history of the entire Western Hemisphere, of which the United States are but a part."[7]

The term has evolved and has expanded to mean a place of intimate relations and territorial limitations where life has been shaped and continues to be shaped by the conquest of the war of 1848. As a result of this war, North American troops invaded and then annexed thousands of miles of Mexican land, thereby incorporating the residents of that land into the larger North American reality. So it should not be surprising that between 1890 and 1930, more than an eighth of Mexico's population came to the United States.[8] The border, a political creation, did not deter the movement of a people who had for centuries crossed a river that now for the first time separated two nations but could not separate or put an end to the ties of family, culture, language, and religion. However, what this new border did create was a buffer zone that in many ways absorbed immigrants in their journey farther north. This *zona fronteriza* (frontier zone) became a magnet for unskilled labor and throughout the twentieth century became a geographical space of great poverty and misery, and not just on the southern side of the Rio Grande.

The borderlands, therefore, can be said to be a tumultuous zone where the Mexican and the indigenous were conquered by the Anglo-European, thus creating a reality of hybrid languages, an amalgamation of traditions and customs, the often violent clash of ideologies and values, a disparate economic system that produces poverty, and a corridor of cultural interaction rich in ambiguities and contradictions. Chicana feminist, poet, and activist Gloria Anzaldúa describes the borderlands: "The U.S.-Mexico border *es una herida abierta* [is an open wound] where the Third World grates against the first and bleeds. And before a scab forms it hemorrhages again, the life blood of two worlds merging to form a third country—a border culture. . . . A borderlands is a vague and undetermined place created by the emotional residue of an unnatural boundary."[9] This "border culture" that Anzaldúa refers to has the unique characteristic of hybridization, called *mestizaje* in Spanish, that is, a confluence of the extremes and disparities that converge in borderlands life and become the reality of a possible third culture. This third culture is built upon a framework of diverse contrasts and experiences. It is a culture that encompasses economic polarization, underlying racial politics, cultural adaptation, and cultural fusion such as intermarriages, holiday traditions, and religious observances. In the borderlands life is lived in a social environment that is strongly configured by a very extensive system of mutual borrowing.

Added to this understanding of the borderlands are the demographics and economic realities of the border region, which in turn affect the entire country. The population is increasing by 3 percent per year on the U.S. side and 4 percent per year on the Mexican side. Projections are that this border population will continue to grow to 36 million persons by the year 2020 (30 million on the Mexican side and 6.3 million on the U.S. side). Currently the four fastest growing cities in the state of Texas are the border cities of Laredo, Brownsville, McAllen, and El Paso.

What do these demographic and economic realities mean? They mean that in the borderlands the most significant reality is life in the margins. The margins of society can be experienced as economic, social, cultural, linguistic, racial, and religious. The borderlands are all about belonging and not belonging; about centers and margins; about national identity and national rejection; about how others see the Latina/o community and also how they interpret our existence. In response to this, Latinas/os become daily border crossers who must learn early on to interpret life on both sides—life in the dominant culture and life in the Latina/o community. This is how we learn to survive and how we are able to be who we really are, and it is this very paradox of belonging yet not really belonging where the history and life of Latinas/os begins to be understood, not just nationally but also within our own denominational histories, as Protestants and as Roman Catholics. It is also where we need to begin our analysis of what this paradox implies for the twenty-first-century United States. There is indeed a demographic "browning" of this country taking place. Demographers estimate that the Latina/o population will grow from its present census figure of about 35 million to approximately 46 million in 2025 or almost 25 percent of the total U.S. population.

While it is true that Latinas/os are a mosaic of pigmentation and *mestizaje*, and while it is true that there is a distinctiveness to our cultures, once we enter the shores of this nation we share a common history and we are imagined by the larger culture in particular ways. In *This Bridge Called My Back* Gloria Anzaldúa says about this external imagining of who Latinas/os are: "Who, me confused? Ambivalent? Not so. Only your labels split me."[10] We were removed, we were split from the category of Caucasian—something the Jews and Italians and Germans and Irish and Swedes never stopped being. The Latina/o history is in many ways similar to the story of all immigrants but it is also different in very particular ways. Latinas/os represent the reality of the third world most North Americans would rather forget. But this reality cannot be forgotten because the truth is that the third world is no longer "over there," across a vast ocean (east or west), but is right across the street.

## THE BORDERLANDS AND GLOBALIZATION

Let me invite you now to think about globalization. First we are confronted with its concrete and economic manifestations, which are, of course, very significant. For example, we must acknowledge that multinational corporations do have the potential to influence both political and economic life in all corners of the globe. According to *Forbes Magazine,* the largest multinational corporations, such as General Motors, Ford, and Mitsubishi, enjoy total sales that exceed the gross domestic product of all but the most productive nations in the world. It is almost beyond comprehension that foreign currency exchange totals $1.5 trillion per day and that this figure dwarfs the global trade of products.[11] This is the numerical side of globalization that is very important and merits careful analysis. As practitioners of our Christian faith, however, I want us to examine another equally important side of globalization. We must also understand that globalization "itself has been a long-term process extending over many centuries, although only in recent centuries has it, with increasing rapidity, assumed a particular, discernible form."[12]

In order to move toward a faith-inspired vision of globalization, however, we must ask one very basic but crucial question: Who are the victims of globalization? More specifically, who are the victims of globalization in the borderlands? We ask the question because of two important Christian concerns, the unity of the human family and the reality of the poor in the context of our lived reality. And our concern develops from our understanding that the Christian community has been called and enabled by God to be defenders of what is just and to be instruments to promote that justice right here where we live. I think what has become clear is that "the benefits of globalization do not extend to all countries or social groups. Indeed, the dramatic extremes of wealth and poverty born of globalization menace both democracy and social stability in various regions [of the world]."[13] This is shown by the fact that "by some estimates roughly a fifth of the world's population lives in absolute poverty, bringing fear, early death, squalid living conditions, and disease."[14]

As we think about the ethical/religious side of globalization and we look at how it affects life in the borderlands, we become aware of what demands are being made of those who take seriously the profound questions of distributive justice. As we consider the reality of life in the borderlands we must also consider the human persons, cultural forces, social processes, historical context, and economic institutions that influence how globalization is experienced in this corner of the world. The Tejanos of today still face higher levels of poverty, disease, unemployment, and violence than do other residents of the state. Race and language continue to be controversial and emotional issues for the residents of this state as does the issue of immigration. When we factor in the forces of globalization we realize the negative impact it is having on this borderlands region as new residents move to the south Texas/border area.

On the U.S. side we find the reality of the *colonias,* which are unincorporated rural settlements. A June 1987 *Newsweek* article called these *colonias* "rural slums," "prisons of poverty," "a grim new Appalachia," and the "worst the U.S. has to offer";[15] and the sad reality is that the *colonia* is a unique south Texas/border phenomenon. While rural poverty exists elsewhere in the nation, *colonias* do not. These unincorporated settlements are too far away from cities to connect to sewer systems, water systems, and electrical systems, and they do not have the benefit of other municipal services such as trash collection. Of the 868 *colonias* counted by the Texas Water Development Board in 1995, more than 750 of them lacked wastewater connections and 204 did not have access to treated water.[16] Unemployment is high, as is the dropout rate for high school students. Flooding is a constant threat in most of the *colonias* as is insect and rodent infestation. In research done by a team from the University of Texas–Pan American, of the *colonia* households they interviewed 90 percent had incomes less than $15,000 a year and 62 percent had incomes less than $9,000 a year.[17] Yet the researchers also discovered that 77 percent of the respondents owned their own homes, or 14 percent said a family member owned the home.[18] Although we are surely talking about very modest homes built with a variety of inexpensive materials, the point is that the *colonia* resident continues a long tradition of home ownership that also enables her/him to maintain ties to Mexico while living in the United States. But more than that, because most *colonia* residents have no access to health insurance and cannot afford U.S. medical care, proximity to the border is also a matter of survival. They can go to Mexico for low-cost medical care and can also purchase prescription drugs in Mexico without a prescription. Many *colonia* residents work on both sides of the border, and being able to cross back and forth is in many cases a "matter of survival for those at the bottom of the social order."[19] Like the rest of the borderlands, the *colonia* resident can be a U.S. citizen, a U.S. resident, or an undocumented alien.

Of course, *colonias* also exist on the other side of the river in Mexico. Here the *colonias* are mostly made up of *maquiladora* workers. If you ever want to touch and feel the power of globalization all you have to do is visit any *maquiladora* complex in Matamoros, Ciudad Júarez, or Tijuana. These very large assembly plants are located all along the Mexico-U.S. border in Mexico. Today there are more than 4,000 *maquilas* in Mexico that produce everything from garments to automobiles to dialysis equipment to computer motherboards to athletic shoes to women's underwear, mainly for the U.S. market. Most of the plants are owned by U.S. companies, but there is also investment capital from Germans, Koreans, Japanese, and Mexicans. These transnational corporations set up in Mexico primarily for "cheap labor," and it shows in the lives of the more than one million *maquiladora* workers, whose meager wages leave them far below the Mexican poverty level. Many companies also come for lax environmental enforcement, and that shows, too, in the widespread industrial pollution plaguing many border cities.[20] The in-bound *maquiladora* or twin plant program was established by the Mexican government in 1965 as the Border Industrialization Plan. This program allowed foreign companies to establish highly competitive manufacturing and production facilities in Mexico and to ship raw materials and components to those facilities under special tariffs or oftentimes tariff-free.[21]

When I started teaching seminary in Texas, I decided to include a trip with students to the border region as part of a course I teach on the Latina/o church in the borderlands. On these trips we "immerse" ourselves in the everyday lives of the people. I have been visiting *colonias* for more than ten years now and I am always troubled by the poverty and living conditions that we encounter on every immersion trip. In addition to the water and sewer problems already mentioned, many *colonias* are also affected by the danger of pesticide contamination as nearby fields are sprayed by crop dusters. However, I have always been struck by the deep sense of hope that I have encountered over and over again in the *colonia* residents I have met. Despite dismal surroundings, they have a great hope that life will improve, and this hope is fed by a vibrant faith. As my students and I stand in the yards of these families, staring at the simple one- or two-room dwellings; as we notice the use of car batteries to power a small television set or see a collection of brightly colored flowers along a fence built with discarded pieces of wood; as chickens and children run and play all around us, we are forced to look in the faces of the people standing before us and see ourselves. These women and men are our sisters and brothers. These women and men also love God and want to seek God's love and mercy and protection. I am always humbled when we are asked to say a blessing for the family and their home. The challenge is for us to see the value and worth of the people who stand before us. The challenge is to acknowledge the *imago Dei* in their faces.

The many *maquiladora* workers I have met through the years share a similar story: they work 40–50 hours per week for a salary that can run anywhere from $25 to $50 U.S. Over 80 percent are women from the ages of 16 to 24 and sexual harassment as well as loss of employment because of pregnancy is common. I have met workers who have been contaminated by exposure to chemicals and as a result have been either blinded or have developed seizures; some of the women we have met have developed cancer; needless to say these workers have access to very poor medical care and most have no workers' compensation. In the *maquiladoras* there is little concern to provide workers with safety equipment such as industrial masks or gloves since it seems that as soon as one worker becomes ill and is dismissed, another is there to take her or his place.

In the many conversations I have had with these young *maquiladora* workers, teenagers in most cases, the plea has been the same. They tell me: "We do not want to make as much as workers in the United States, we want to earn a just wage. We want to make enough money so that we may have enough to eat, to feed our families, to provide for our needs." I met a young mother of a two-year-old who had never been able to buy a quart of milk, since milk is a luxury along the border. I met a young couple who wanted to save enough to buy small glass panes to put in the windows they had made that were covered up by cardboard. They wanted real windows that would keep the air out of their small shack and still let the sunlight in. The majority of these workers come from the interior of Mexico. Again and again we were asked to pray for their families, for their efforts to organize as workers within the *maquiladoras*, to pray that God would give them courage to speak up against the many injustices they faced in their jobs. I saw devastating poverty and great economic injustice, but I never heard words of hate. Instead there were warm smiles and the acknowledgment that God was their ultimate source of comfort. These women and men shared what little they owned in an effort to help a neighbor. They opened the doors of their very simple houses and made us feel welcome, often apologizing that they could not offer us something to drink or to eat.

This is the reality we face as borderlands residents, and it is in this context that the church in the borderlands has been called to serve. In this reality the church community is challenged to live its faith and to make real the Jesus of Nazareth, who the Gospels tell us was moved to compassion. Although compassion is not considered a very valuable sentiment in globalization, it is at the core of Christian behavior. Compassion allows us to see the *imago Dei* in the faces of those not like us and it gives us the strength to reach out to those we consider foreign, other, and to attempt to build community. The strong sense of relationships, of friendships, of support found in the *colonias* of south Texas and in the *colonias* alongside the *maquiladora* plants in Mexico seems to condemn the great individualism that pervades the lifestyle we have in this country today. Our society has been invaded by an individualism that fractures our lives and creates competition and alienation rather than cooperation and relationships. In an article about globalization and the need for the universalization of human values, Spanish theologian José Ignacio González Faus said that in a department store in Barcelona he came across a sign that read, "I consume, therefore I am." This sign, he says, is an example of how purely economic globalization has created the figure of "homo consumptor": "consumerism is not a natural human trait but a cultural construct created artificially."[22] It is represented by the emergence of a common consumer culture obtained via an aggressive advertising that is worldwide, and he sees this push to create consumers as one of the main characteristics of an economic globalization that ultimately produces structures of inhumanity that denigrate and oppress.

Dehumanization is key for consumerism to flourish and economic inequity to grow. A United Nations report shows that relative earnings of rich and poor were 30 to 1 in 1960, 60 to 1 in 1990, and 74 to 1 in 1997. These figures show that there is no "planetary concern for the existence of a 'human family.'"[23] Theologian Jon Sobrino says, "How to succeed in being one human 'family' on a planet where some small minorities take life for granted while life is the one thing the great majorities cannot take for granted is the basic question global-ization has to answer."[24]

For Sobrino, the answer to this troubling question is solidarity. He defines solidarity as closeness, support, and defense of the weak. "Solidarity is the ten-derness of peoples."[25] Solidarity, Sobrino holds, is the strongest critique of glob-alization. Solidarity represents "support among unequals, with all giving and receiving the best they all have at all levels."[26] This solidarity will produce close-ness instead of distance, appreciation in place of the contempt usually shown to those who have come in without being asked, and joy in place of the fear that those who have come in will take over.[27]

## CONCLUSION

So how is God calling us to respond to the issues of injustice that predominate in the borderlands? One of the basic needs most folks have when trying to understand these complex issues is information, and the good news is that many other committed folks are already out there involved and willing to share their information with us. Take the time to read as much as you can about the *maquiladora* industry; find out about health hazards caused by poverty and environmental pollution; and learn about the economic realities of border life in the United States and Mexico. If you feel that you really want to volunteer and have firsthand experience, do it! Most organizations are prepared to work with volunteers and have in-house educational opportunities, so take the time to call, go online, read—be informed and don't be afraid to ask, but most of all don't be afraid to get involved.

Christianity has historically argued for the intrinsic worth of the human per-son and has made a distinction between intrinsic worth and instrumental worth. This means that when facing an economic globalization that sees humans as objects to be commodified, whose value is based on how much they can produce and contribute to the profit margin, Christians must stand in opposition and call on values that connect the human person to God and there-fore to her or his intrinsic worth. Christians must continue to advocate for an interpretation of human life that is mediated through beliefs about and experi-ences of the living God, the God of Jesus Christ. William Schweiker puts it this way: "Any cultural force or social institution that nullifies our sense of the real-ity of justice and mercy is, practically speaking, atheistic, and theoretically stated, nihilistic. If that is true of our global situation, then Christians must advocate ways of containing and constraining transnational corporations."[28] Schweiker understands that this is a complex task because it involves more than simply establishing the rational necessity of God or a concept of the Good. It is a hermeneutical, cultural problem, namely, how to fill our self-understand-ing with beliefs about the worth of persons and the claims of justice.[29]

Therefore the task facing the church is that it must transmit this picture of the worth of human life and enable that picture to penetrate the global, social imagination.[30] We are called to be agents of change. We are called to be examples of empathy and compassion. We are called to see ourselves in the faces of those who live on the margins and on the bottom. We are called to celebrate the claim that all human beings are God's beloved children. We are called to transmit the depth of meaning of the South African proverb: "A person becomes a person through other persons."[31] The Christian community is continually called to work to establish links of solidarity. We must come together so that as a Christian people we can confront the misconception that globalization is only an economic phenomenon and be willing and prepared to examine its moral and spiritual dimensions. We must come together and in one voice affirm the "humanity of all peoples and to uphold their right to the conditions needed to preserve their humanity."[32]

## QUESTIONS FOR DISCUSSION

1. Given the current and projected demographics of our society, what are the ways in which U.S. culture and public policy will need to change in response to an increased Latino/a population? How should our local congregations respond to the shifting population in our country? What about our denomination?

2. Find out some of the ways that economic globalization and specific economic policies are causing people to migrate from poor countries, and specifically how this affects your local community and state. What local policies might you and your congregation work to change? What national policies? How can we be in solidarity with migrants and people in the borderlands?

3. In defining the term "borderlands" Machado introduces a broader approach to American history that is not simply Anglo-oriented or limited to the thirteen colonies. What difference would it make to think about American history not just in terms of movement westward from British America, but also northward from Spanish America?

## RESOURCES

### Books and Articles

Anzaldúa, Gloria E., and Analouise Keating. *This Bridge We Call Home: Radical Visions for Transformation.* New York: Routledge, 2002.
Aquino, Maria Pilar, Daisy L. Machado, and Jeanette Rodriguez. *A Reader in Latina Feminist Theology: Religion and Justice.* Austin: University of Texas Press, 2002.

Kamel, Rachael, and Anya Hoffman, eds. *The Maquiladora Reader: Cross-Border Organizing Since NAFTA.* Philadelphia: American Friends Service Committee, 1999.

Louie, Miriam Ching Yoon. *Sweatshop Warriors: Immigrant Women Workers Take on the Global Factory.* Cambridge, MA: South End Press, 2001.

Nevins, Joseph. *Operation Gatekeeper: The Rise of the Illegal Alien and the Making of the U.S.–Mexico Boundary.* New York: Routledge, 2001.

Walker, Randi Jones. "Liberators for Colonial Anáhuac: A Rumination on North American Civil Religions." *Religion and American Culture* 9, no. 2 (1999): 183–203.

### Organizations and Web Sites

Good Samaritan Ministries. www.swgsm.org/English.

Proyecto Azteca. www.bordercoalition.org/Proyecto%20Azteca.

Borderlinks. www.borderlinks.org.

Humane Borders. www.humaneborders.org.

Coalition for Justice in the Maquiladoras. www.coalitionforjustice.net/index.html.

National Immigration Forum. www.immigrationforum.org.

### Videos and DVDs

*Forgotten Americans.* KLRU Television. 2000.

*Señorita Extraviada.* Independent Television Service. 2001.

# NOTES

1. See David M. Reimers, *Unwelcome Strangers: American Identity and the Turn Against Immigration* (New York: Columbia University Press, 1998), 5.
2. Ibid., 9.
3. Ibid., 17, 18.
4. Ibid., 21.
5. John Francis Bannon, *Bolton and the Spanish Borderlands* (Norman: University of Oklahoma Press, 1964), 3.
6. Ibid.
7. Herbert E. Bolton, "Defensive Spanish Expansion and the Significance of the Borderlands," *Wider Horizons of American History* (New York: Appleton-Century, 1939), 56.
8. James D. Cockcroft, *Latinos in the Making of the United States* (New York: Franklin Watts, 1995), 13.
9. Gloria Anzaldúa, *Borderlands/La Frontera* (San Francisco: Aunt Lute Press, 1987), 3.
10. "La Prieta," in *This Bridge Called My Back: Writings by Radical Women of Color,* ed. Cherríe Moraga and Gloria Anzaldúa, 2nd ed. (Latham, NY: Kitchen Table, Women of Color Press, 1983), 205.
11. Douglas A. Hicks, "Thinking Globally," *The Christian Century,* December 12, 2001, 14.
12. Roland Robertson, "Globalization and the Future of 'Traditional Religion,'" in *God and Globalization, vol. 1: Religion and the Powers of the Common Life,* ed. Max Stackhouse and Peter Paris (Harrisburg: Trinity Press International, 2000), 53–54.
13. Yersu Kim, "Philosophy and the Prospects for a Universal Ethics," in ibid., 77.
14. William Schweiker, "Responsibility in the World of Mammon," in ibid., 105.

15. Cited in Chad Richardson, *Batos, Bolillos, Pochos, and Pelados* (Austin: University of Texas Press, 1999), 43.
16. Ibid., 53.
17. Ibid., 50.
18. Ibid., 45.
19. Ibid., 52.
20. www.americas.org/news/Features/CJM's_10-year_anniversary.html.
21. www.tnrcc.state.tx.us/exec/oppr/border/border.html.
22. José Ignacio González Faus, "The Utopia of the Human Family," *Concilium 2001/5, Globalization and Its Victims,* ed. Jon Sobrino and Felix Wilfred (London: SCM, 2001), 100.
23. Jon Sobrino, "Redeeming Globalization through Its Victims," in ibid., 111.
24. Ibid.
25. Ibid.
26. Ibid.
27. Ibid.
28. Schweiker, "Responsibility," 129.
29. Ibid., 132.
30. Ibid., 133.
31. Donald W. Shriver Jr., "The Taming of Mars," in Stackhouse and Paris, *Religion and the Powers,* 156.
32. Peter Paris, "Moral Exemplars in the Global Community," in *God and Globalization,* vol. 2: *The Spirit and the Modern Authorities,* ed. Max Stackhouse and Don S. Browning (Harrisburg: Trinity Press International, 2001), 210.

# Chapter 10

# Reforming Global Economic Policies

*Pamela K. Brubaker*

> *The spirituality of life, which is basic to our Christian faith, is intrinsically at odds with prevailing political-economic arrangements and policies that are creating and exacerbating human suffering. Therefore, we believe that, eventually, nothing less than a fundamental shift in political-economic paradigms is necessary for humankind to become instruments of God in striving for the vision of just, participatory and sustainable communities.[1]*

I first became aware of these arrangements and policies when I participated in a United Nations Decade for Women conference in Nairobi, Kenya, in 1985. Over 15,000 women from around the world participated in the nongovernmental forum that ran parallel to the official conference. In plenary sessions and workshops I heard women from Africa, Asia, and Latin America report how structural adjustment programs imposed by the World Bank and International Monetary Fund (IMF) as conditions for loans were increasing the suffering of people in their countries. A typical program required countries to orient their agriculture and other production for export. This ensured that countries would earn foreign currency to repay their loans. But it also meant that land that had been used for domestic food consumption was now used to grow crops like coffee and cocoa for export. Countries also had to open their markets to international corporations and change trade policies that favored their own producers. This contributed to job loss as it was difficult for local producers to compete with large foreign corporations. Another requirement was the privatization of state-owned concerns, which meant that income from these industries now went to private corporations rather than the public budget.

Deregulation—removing worker and environmental protections—was also required. In addition, countries had to cut social spending on education and health care. These policies led to dramatic drops in living standards. Malnutrition and child mortality rates increased. Health care was unaffordable for many families. Children, particularly girls, left school, for their families could not afford the fees. Women's burdens increased as their hours of unpaid work lengthened to help their families survive.

These policies—forms of liberalization, privatization, and deregulation—are advocated by those who support what is called neoliberalism, the prevailing political-economic paradigm of the last two decades. Neoliberalism looks to private capital and "free markets" to allocate resources and promote growth. Margaret Thatcher and Ronald Reagan led the campaign for countries to adopt these polices, which would supposedly contribute to economic growth and development. Although some countries like India and China have experienced growth and development, many others have not. The World Bank and IMF continue to impose these measures, even though structural adjustment policies have been replaced with "poverty reduction strategy papers" as requirements for loans.[2] Overall, these policies have widened the gap between the wealthy and the poor, exploited the earth's resources at an unsustainable rate, and increased pollution and social exclusion. A sobering statistic is that the total income of the richest 1 percent of the global population is equal to that of the poorest 57 percent, and at least 24,000 people die every day from poverty and malnutrition.[3]

Since the countries of the global north are primarily responsible for shaping the policies of the World Bank and IMF, women from the global south at the conference challenged the women from the global north to study and action. During the two decades since this event, I have learned more about the World Bank and IMF, and the role of the U.S. government in setting their policies. In the first part of this chapter, I sketch the story of these institutions and the impact of their policies. I then outline an alternative political-economic paradigm and strategies for transforming the current paradigm toward a more just and sustainable one. My discussion draws on my participation in recent encounters (2003–2004) between the World Council of Churches (WCC), the IMF, and the World Bank—encounters that were initiated by the IMF.[4]

Justice and care—two of the values inherent in a spirituality oriented toward life—are the ethical basis of my discussion. Economist William K. Tabb asserts: "We must always remember this central aspect of the nature of capitalism—it is always a process of redistributive growth."[5] Thus I am particularly concerned about distributive justice, which asks about the community's distribution of benefits and burdens. Who benefits from the process? Who suffers? Is the process equitable? The value of care emphasizes the importance of all the activities—unpaid and paid—that keep daily life functioning. This reminds us of a broader understanding of economics, one that includes both production and social reproduction: the provisioning of life and care for the earth. This understanding of economics, grounded in Christian faith, was shared by Adam Smith in his groundbreaking work, *The Wealth of Nations.* The current paradigm I describe below looks to Smith but has narrowed his understanding of economics to market exchange.

## THE CURRENT PARADIGM OF ECONOMIC GLOBALIZATION

The World Bank and the IMF were established in 1944 to lead the postwar push to globalize the world's economies, with the stated aim of promoting peace and prosperity. The Bank was to provide the capital to reconstruct and develop war-torn nations. After this was accomplished, it focused on loans to developing countries. The IMF promoted cooperation on monetary policies, exchange rate stability, and the expansion of world trade. An International Trade Organization was also proposed. However, its creation was blocked by the U.S. Congress, who thought it would harm U.S. interests. (It was seen as too friendly to labor and "third world" countries.) The General Agreement on Tariffs and Trade (GATT) was organized in its place. GATT was a framework for ongoing negotiations on reduction in tariffs to expand trade. It evolved into the World Trade Organization (WTO), established in 1995, as the international institution responsible for setting and enforcing the rules of trade.

My participation in the encounters with the World Bank and IMF confirmed the charge that the U.S government, particularly the Treasury Department, uses these institutions as instruments of domination. The U.S. government, in conjunction with the other countries in the G-7 (Canada, Germany, France, Great Britain, Italy, and Japan), plays a crucial role in setting trade and finance policy in these global institutions. Both the World Bank and the IMF have a voting system based mainly on the value of the shares held by its member countries. Because the United States owns the largest number of shares in the Bank and the IMF, it effectively has veto power in both institutions, which it uses to protect U.S. interests.[6] Although in theory the WTO is more democratic, as each country has one vote, a power analysis indicates otherwise. Critics charge that developed countries and transnational corporations skew the agenda. Corporations lobby their governments to press for trade rules that will benefit them. Representatives from developed countries meet outside plenary sessions to make decisions about trade rules, which they then pressure other representatives to accept.

As congressional blockage of the proposed trade organization suggests, there is a tension in the United States between protecting U.S. interests (identified to a large extent with business) and our commitment to global peace and prosperity. A particularly illuminating example is the recommendation from U.S. State Department staff in 1948: "We have 50% of the world's wealth, but only 6.3% of its population. In this situation, our real job in the coming period is to maintain this position of disparity." They added that to do this, "we have to dispense with all sentimentality. We should cease thinking about human rights, the raising of living standards, and democratization."[7] In other words, there is to be *no redistribution of the world's wealth*, which arguably might be crucial to peace and prosperity. Ideals such as human rights, democracy, development—ideals held by many Americans—are dismissed as "sentimental."

The U.S. government has certainly not stopped talking about human rights, democratization, or raising living standards (development). However, an examination of our actual foreign policy suggests that maintaining a grossly disproportionate share of global wealth may continue to be a primary objective. This, I suspect, is often the aim behind more general talk about "national interest" or "the American way of life." It has shaped much of the foreign policy of both Democratic and Republican administrations in the postwar period.

## A BRIEF HISTORICAL REVIEW

During the 1950s, '60s, and early '70s, the U.S. Central Intelligence Agency (CIA) overthrew democratically elected governments in countries such as Guatemala, Iran, the Congo, and Chile. Although the stated rationale was to stop the spread of communism, the historical record (including the CIA's own files) shows that the interests of U.S. transnational corporations were often a crucial factor in these interventions. In Guatemala, for instance, the United Fruit Company objected to proposed land reform policies. The plan of the Guatemalan government would have compensated the company for unused land taken from it at its declared taxable worth. United Fruit demanded 25 times more. Its main shareholders lobbied Alan Dulles, head of the CIA, to overthrow Guatemala's government. Despite the fact that the World Bank supported land reform in Guatemala, the CIA and the Eisenhower administration overthrew the government of President Arbenz and helped select his successor, who dismantled the land reform program.[8] The 1954 CIA coup there led to decades of repression and civil war, in which more than 200,000 civilians were killed by U.S.-government-supported troops and militia.

The U.S. National Security Agency developed other strategies during the 1970s to control countries without CIA intervention, according to John Perkins in his *Confessions of an Economic Hit Man*. The U.S. government pushed for large loans to developing countries, knowing they could not be repaid. Perkins's job, as chief economist for a private consulting firm, was to provide unrealistic projections of economic growth to justify the loans. A condition of these loans was that huge U.S. firms like Bechtel receive the contracts for projects financed

by the loans. The primary beneficiaries of these loans were powerful U.S. corporations and elites in both the United States and the borrowing country.
Perkins calls this arrangement "corporatocracy."[9]

In the 1980s, when interest rates rose and prices for commodities like coffee and cocoa dropped, many countries were unable to pay off their loans. This
came to be called "the third-world debt crisis." The World Bank and the IMF
stepped in with new loans, conditioned on structural adjustment policies
(SAPs), mentioned earlier. SAPs were imposed on over one hundred developing countries. These polices, which were intended to promote neoliberal reform
of national economies, caused significant human suffering but did not reduce
the debt burden.

## CONSEQUENCES OF THE DEBT CRISIS

According to the World Bank, the external debts of all developing countries have
grown from $554 billion in 1980 to $2.4 trillion in 2003. This fourfold increase
occurred even though these countries have made some $5.2 trillion in debt pay-
ments over the intervening twenty-three years. In the period from 1997 to 2003,
the average annual outflow of debt service (i.e., interest and principal payments
in excess of new loans) has amounted to $77 billion. This arrangement can be
described as a redistribution of wealth from poor indebted countries to wealthy
creditors. It is an unjust arrangement that violates principles of distributive justice based on equity, since the distribution of benefits and costs are grossly
inequitable. Furthermore, since the well-being of both humans and the earth
have suffered in the process, the debt crisis is also a violation of the value of care.

The amount of money paid by poor countries for debt service takes a huge
toll. Jubilee U.S.A. points out that the poorest countries are siphoning off
urgently needed resources for health care and education to pay the wealthiest
countries and institutions interest on a debt that they have already paid three
times over. This in a world where AIDS is claiming more than eight thousand
lives a day and literacy rates are falling. Many African nations are of particular
concern as they are at the center of both the debt and the AIDS crisis. Some of
these countries are also suffering from drought and famine and just recovering
from regional conflict. In spite of this reality, African nations pay more in debt
service (interest) to the United States and other creditors than they receive in
new loans, aid, or investment.[10]

Niger provides an example of the negative impact of debt. Zenithou is a
three-year-old fighting a disease caused by common mouth bacteria. This disease, which can be treated with simple antibiotics and mouthwash, eats through
facial muscles, tissue, and bones. Zenithou's family did not have the money to
pay for treatment. Fees are attached to even basic health care as a condition for
debt relief and new loans.[11]

## RESPONSE TO THE DEBT CRISIS

The debt cancellation movement has rightly contended that debt relief would provide funds to help countries reduce poverty and improve living standards. Although in 2005 the Bush administration spoke of 100 percent debt cancellation for the poorest countries, it used U.S. veto power to block a debt restructuring mechanism proposed by the IMF in 2003. This mechanism would have permitted debtor countries to make a case for the reduction or cancellation of their debts. However, it would not have permitted consideration of the question of "odious" or illegitimate debt. The United States argued that canceling such debt would violate the "sanctity of contracts."

Many of these debts were contracted by dictatorships and never used for the benefit of the people. Creditors often knew that the loan money would likely be stolen by the government, but lent it anyway. These are called "odious debts."[12] Interestingly the United States first invoked the doctrine of "odious debts" so that Cuba would not have to pay its debts after the Spanish-American War ended (1898). The Bush administration has invoked this doctrine again to ask for the cancellation of Iraq's debts. It seems that the U.S. government applies this doctrine selectively, to suit "our" interests rather than objective standards of justice.

The U.S. government also blocked creation of an international tax organization that was proposed as one measure to finance development. This organization would have developed a system of transfers from the richest to the poorest regions of the world. A small tax on currency transactions is one example. The United States continues to oppose any type of measures that institutionalize global redistribution of wealth from the rich to the poor. Instead, the United States advocates market expansion and foreign trade as the solution to poverty. This is the development model supported in the current round of WTO negotiations. The IMF and World Bank have been instructed by their boards to support this approach, in the interest of "policy coherence." In other words, their development policies must continue to stress market expansion and foreign trade so as to fit with the approach of the WTO.

During the encounters between the WCC, the World Bank and the IMF in which I participated, Bank and IMF staff presented studies that showed that market expansion and foreign trade enhanced economic development. They seemed not to be aware of a well-regarded study by a World Bank economist that demonstrated that openness to foreign trade had an especially negative impact on poor and middle-income groups in poor countries.[13] At times we experienced a degree of arrogance by some staff. For instance, when we cited Joseph Stiglitz's critique of IMF policies at a September 2003 encounter, an IMF director stated that "just because Joe Stiglitz won a Nobel Prize in economics does not mean that he understands the policies of the IMF." Interestingly, in March of 2003 the IMF had released a study by its chief economist that confirmed Stiglitz's criticism of IMF recommendations for opening financial markets to foreign investment. "The empirical evidence has not established a definitive proof that financial integration has enhanced growth for developing countries." In addition, the study found that financial integration "may be associated with higher consumption vulnerability."[14] In other words, financial integration—opening one's economy to more foreign investment—may make it more difficult for poorer people to meet their basic needs.

This has certainly been the case with Mexico since its entry into the North American Free Trade Agreement (NAFTA). For example, many small farmers have been pushed off their land. Jose Magdaleno, a corn producer from the Chiapas region, reports that corn grown in the United States and sold cheaply in Mexico is squeezing out small producers like him. Communities in Chiapas that have successfully grown corn for thousands of years are unable to compete with the subsidized corn from the United States.[15] Some of these people see no option for supporting their families but to cross into the United States without proper immigration documents. Over three thousand people have died trying to cross the U.S.-Mexican border since NAFTA was implemented in 1994.

## AN ALTERNATIVE PARADIGM

The negative impacts of neoliberal globalization are often literally a matter of life and death. Less deadly impacts, like increasing the difficulty poor people face in meeting their basic needs, violate the values of justice and care. Negative impacts on gender equality strategies, the environment, working conditions and labor laws, and overall economic development also violate these values. The building of democratic societies is threatened by corporate-led globalization, growing inequalities, and concentration of economic power. The neoliberal economic paradigm should be of particular concern to all of us who are committed to democracy, and to gender, social, and ecological justice. Christians are called to work in solidarity with others to transform structures and policies that cause suffering and death.

The biblical Sabbath-Jubilee vision is an inspiration to some who are looking for an alternative political economic paradigm to corporate-led globalization. Every seventh (Sabbath) year, the land is to rest and lie fallow, "so that the poor of your people may eat" (Exodus 23:10–12). During this year debts are to be released, so that "there will . . . be no one in need among you" (Deuteronomy 15:1–5). The Jubilee tradition (Leviticus 25:1–55; 27:16–24; Isaiah 61; Luke 4) adds a new feature to the Sabbath year. During the fiftieth year, the land is to be returned to the families who lost it because of poverty and debt. Thus the "Jubilee fully restores the access by the poor to the resources of production and well-being. It goes far beyond distributive justice to restitution of people's capacity and means to provide for life."[16] In short, these traditions point to transformation of uneven and unjust relations.

The WCC, a fellowship of over three hundred Orthodox and Protestant denominations from over one hundred countries, has long been involved in economic issues and development programs. Economic globalization has been a particular focus since 1998, when delegates to the WCC Eighth Assembly called on the ecumenical community to address and remedy the suffering that globalization was causing their communities. Since then the WCC has held several regional consultations on economic globalization, in conjunction with the World Alliance of Reformed Churches and the Lutheran World Federation. This work resulted in a common critique of neoliberal globalization and the development of an alternative paradigm, called an "economy of life."

An economy of life calls for a world of just, participatory, and sustainable communities. A full description of the vision can be found in "Alternative Globalization Addressing Peoples and Earth" (AGAPE), a background document for the Ninth Assembly of the WCC in February 2006. A crucial element of this alternative paradigm is to make "people's work, knowledge and creativity" the driving forces of economic activity, rather than capital owned and controlled by a small, extremely wealthy elite.[17] There is a place for markets in this alternative, but they are not the final arbiter of value. For example, water is a basic need and public good that should not be reduced to a commodity to be bought and sold for profit. An economy of life seeks to promote cooperation among individuals, communities, and nations, rather than competition. This paradigm gives greater material and moral value to care work, and addresses the gender imbalances associated with care work.[18]

Finance and trade are also addressed by this alternative paradigm. It claims that the purpose of an international financial system should be to enhance justice, eradicate poverty, and sustain the environment. Current policies and practices, such as liberalization and deregulation, encourage financial speculation. Over $1.9 trillion is traded every day, most of it for speculative purposes. This speculation dominates trade in goods and services, which takes resources away from productive investment aimed at meeting human needs. One way to curb this speculation is to impose a tax on financial transactions or short-term investment. Moving the U.S. government to support this idea is an important long-term strategy. If the money raised from the tax is used by a democratically constituted international organization (not the World Bank or IMF), this could be a significant source of funds for sustainable social and economic development.[19]

Another way to make finance more just is to cancel the debt. In 2005, in response to pressure from the Jubilee movement, the G-8 countries agreed to the principle of 100 percent debt cancellation for eighteen countries. However, there are conditions for cancellation, such as privatization of publicly owned enterprises. Although this plan is an important first step, we must remember that it came about because of the joint commitment and actions of nongovernmental organizations (NGOs), faith communities, and people from around the world. The aim of the Jubilee movement is 100 percent debt cancellation for fifty countries without requiring harmful policies. The JUBILEE Act, a bill Jubilee U.S.A. supports in the U.S. Congress, would do this. Still, the issue of illegitimate and odious debts remains. Here the strategy is to create an independent arbitration panel, under the auspices of the United Nations, to hear claims from nations and NGOs and to negotiate settlements.

A last strategy to promote just finance is to identify and quantify social and ecological debt. Peoples and countries of the global south have suffered immensely from a global economic system that primarily benefits the global north. This reality can be understood in terms of social and ecological debt, which is owed to the south. Examples of ecological debt are World Bank– and IMF-funded large dams, oil and gas pipelines, and other projects that severely damaged the environment of southern countries. A WCC consultation suggests that restitution and reparations should be made to those to whom ecological debt is owed, especially workers, farmers, and indigenous peoples communities. One way to make restitution is for the United States and other G-7 countries to make good on prior commitments of 0.7 percent of gross national income for development assistance, not as an act of charity but as an act of restitution.

This paradigm claims that trade should aim to serve just ends—"ethical, sustainable and equitable production, exchange and consumption of goods and services to meet the needs of all humankind and the earth."[20] It argues for trade that protects human rights and the earth through effective labor and environmental regulations. Developing countries should be able to protect their agricultural sector so as to ensure food security for their people. The campaign against the Free Trade Area of the Americas (FTAA) is a good example. Many religious, human rights, labor, and environmental groups have joined together to oppose this agreement in its current form. It is a form of free trade that encourages competition between unequal partners, a situation that permits more powerful countries to benefit inequitably. For instance, services such as education, health care, water, and electricity are currently included in FTAA negotiations. If these areas are privatized and opened to trade and investment, transnational corporations in the global north will likely be the ones to profit.

Inequities in the global trading system under the rules of the WTO are also a matter of concern. An example is the subsidies given to large corporate farms by the U.S. government that put small farms here and abroad at a competitive disadvantage. In the last decade, the focus of U.S. farm policy has shifted as the government abandoned historically market-stabilizing tools (such as payments to farmers to let some fields lie fallow to reduce overproduction) in favor of trade liberalization (opening markets and reducing tariffs in other countries). This has had drastic consequences for farmers in the United States and around the world, such as a drop of more than 40 percent in world prices for four chief U.S. farm exports—corn, wheat, soybeans, and cotton. At the same time, government payments to farmers have increased, since direct payments are made to farmers whenever prices decline. Small farms are going under even with these payments, while corporate farms expand. "In their wake, farmers from the U.S. to Peru, from Haiti to Burkina Faso have harvested poorer incomes, hunger, desperation and migration."[21] Congressional action is needed here, too, to end unfair farm subsidies.

## CONCLUSION

Organizations such as the Jubilee movement for debt cancellation and the Oxfam "Make Trade Fair" program are working for more just policies and institutions. Most denominations have agencies that focus on economic justice issues as part of their work. These organizations and agencies are excellent sources of information and opportunities for challenging unjust economic policies, particularly in relation to the U.S. government. For instance, Jubilee U.S.A. has a Jubilee Congregation program. In addition, most denominations are part of transnational organizations like the World Alliance of Reformed Churches, the Lutheran World Federation, and the WCC that work cooperatively for ecological and economic justice. These are additional sources for information on global issues.

Individuals or congregations can sign up to receive newsletters and other publications from these organizations. Many also have e-mail action alerts to notify their constituencies of needed action, such as contacting Congress or the White House on legislation for debt cancellation or fair trade. Although it is unusual, delegations have changed the minds of congressional representatives. For example, a conservative congressperson became a leading advocate for debt relief for poor countries after a delegation from his district appealed to him on both religious and pragmatic grounds.

All the chapters in this book suggest strategies that are crucial to moving toward a world of just, sustainable communities. The challenges before us are deep and our efforts often halting. I take heart in those beginning to hear the cries of the suffering and becoming aware of its causes. There is hope in the many communities of resistance and transformation, communities that are themselves living alternatives to corporate-led globalization. Acting in solidarity with those resisting and transforming neoliberal globalization revives ideals of human rights, democracy, and improved living standards. Acting in solidarity gives us a deep sense of community with all peoples and creatures, allowing us to share more fully in a spirituality of life.

# QUESTIONS FOR DISCUSSION

1. Brubaker makes clear that U.S. participation in the policy making of international institutions like the World Bank and IMF have contributed to growing injustice in the two-thirds world. What responsibility do U.S. citizens and congregations have for being involved in dialogues and debates on policies such as structural adjustment, trade agreements, debt relief, and international finance rules? How might you and your congregation participate in promoting justice for the developing world?

2. It is often difficult to imagine that individual citizens, local congregations, or even national denominational bodies can make any difference in changing or shaping national or international public policy. If we live in a democracy, why is it that citizens often feel so disempowered by the political process? What can we do to begin to change our mind-sets and our political processes so that we can become more involved? How do biblical traditions, like the Sabbath-Jubilee Brubaker discusses, help us think about change?

3. Many congregations have gotten involved in buying fair trade coffee and sponsoring alternative Christmas bazaars. What other small-scale strategies can individuals and congregations undertake to address global injustice? How can we go beyond small-scale strategies to push for public policy changes for more just trade?

# RESOURCES

## Books and Articles

Beneria, Lourdes. *Gender, Development, and Globalization: Development as if All People Mattered.* New York: Routledge, 2003.

Duchrow, Ulrich, and Franz J. Hinkelammert. *Property for People, Not for Profit: Alternatives to the Global Tyranny of Capital.* Geneva: World Council of Churches Publications, 2004.

International Forum on Globalization. *Alternatives to Economic Globalization: A Better World Is Possible.* San Francisco: Berrett-Koehler, 2004.

Kinsler, Ross, and Gloria Kinsler. *The Biblical Jubilee and the Struggle for Life.* Maryknoll, NY: Orbis, 1999.

Peralta, Athena K. "A Caring Economy: A Feminist Contribution to Alternatives to Globalization Addressing People and Earth (AGAPE)." Geneva: World Council of Churches, 2005.

World Council of Churches. "Alternative Globalization Addressing Peoples and Earth (AGAPE): A Background Document." Geneva: World Council of Churches, 2005.

## Organizations and Web Sites

International Forum on Globalization. www.ifg.org.

Jubilee debt cancellation movements. www.jubileeusa.org and www.jubileesouth.org.
Justice Platform for Global Development. www.fpif.org/form_justice.sign-on.html.
Oxfam International. www.oxfam.org/eng.
Sabbath Economics. www.sabbatheconomics.org.
World Council of Churches. www.wcc-coe.org/wcc/what/jpc/economy.html.

### Videos and DVDs

*Bill Moyers Report: Trading Democracy.* Public Broadcasting Service. 2002.
*Deadly Embrace: Nicaragua, the World Bank and the IMF.* Global Exchange. 1999.
*Global Village or Global Pillage.* Produced by Jeremy Brecher. 1999.
*Life and Debt.* Tuff Gong Pictures Production. 2001.
*Profits of Doom.* British Broadcasting Corporation. 2001.
*Stolen Childhoods.* Galen Films. 2004.

## NOTES

1. World Council of Churches, "Giving Witness of the Hope That Is in Us: Our Passion for the Possible," Sept. 11–12, 2003. Statement from the WCC Internal Encounter of Churches, Agencies, and other Partners on the World Bank and IMF.

2. In response to criticisms of structural adjustment programs, in 1999 the IMF replaced the Enhanced Structural Adjustment Programs with the Poverty Reduction and Growth Facility (PRGF). Any programs supported by the PRGF are structured around comprehensive, country-owned "Poverty Reduction Strategy Papers." The IMF and World Bank cooperate on these programs, particularly on issues of conditions for loans. Critics charge that although the process of preparing the papers is supposedly "owned" by countries, it is expected that the strategies include export production, liberalization of trade and finance, deregulation, and privatization.

3. Branko Milanovic, "True World Income Distribution, 1988 and 1993: First Calculation Based on Household Surveys Alone," *Economic Journal* 112, no. 476 (2002): 51–92.

4. The WCC resisted describing these meetings as dialogues, since they have been very critical of the policies of the World Bank and the IMF. "Encounter" seems more open to a stance of countering the position of one's conversation partners than does the term "dialogue."

5. William Tabb, *The Amoral Elephant: Globalization and the Struggle for Justice in the Twenty-first Century* (New York: Monthly Review Press, 2001), 28.

6. It is important to note that while the United States has the largest number of shares, this is largely due to the size of our economy. In 2004 the U.S. gross domestic product was over 28 percent of total world output ("World Development Indicators Database," World Bank, 15 July 2005, www.worldbank.org). The United States currently holds 16.4 percent of the shares of the International Bank for Reconstruction and Development, the main bank group. In dollar terms, its share of the IBRD's capital is $31 billion out of a total of $190 billion. In the 2004 fiscal year, the IBRD made $11 billion of new loans, bringing the net total to $110 billion. In its report to Congress, the U.S. Treasury Department noted that $1.7 billion worth of goods and services was procured for U.S. business through World Bank operations in 2004.

7. "Review of Current Trends: U.S. Foreign Policy," *Foreign Relations in the United States* 1, no. 2 (1948): 310–29.
8. For a full account of this coup, see Stephen Schlesinger and Stephen Kinzer, *Bitter Fruit: The Story of the American Coup in Guatemala,* expanded ed. (Cambridge: Harvard University Press, 1999).
9. John Perkins, *Confessions of an Economic Hit Man* (San Francisco: Berrett-Koehler, 2004).
10. Jubilee U.S.A., "Jubilee Educational Packet," http://www.jubileeusa.org/edpacket/SAP.pdf.
11. Zenithou's story is from ibid.
12. For a useful discussion of odious debt and criminal debt, see Jeffrey A. Winters, "Criminal Debt," in *Reinventing the World Bank,* ed. Jonathan R. Pincus and Jeffrey A. Winters (Ithaca, NY: Cornell University Press, 2002): 101–30.
13. Branko Milanovic, "Can We Discern the Effect of Globalization on Income Distribution? Evidence from Household Budget Surveys," WB Policy Research Paper no. 2876 (2002), 12.
14. Eswar Presad, Kenneth Rogoff, Shang-Jin Wei, and M. Ayhan Kose, "Effects of Financial Globalization on Developing Countries: Some Empirical Evidence," International Monetary Fund, March 17, 2003, #114.
15. "Corn in the U.S.A.," http://www.maketradefair.com/en/index.php?file=2103 2002103151.htm.
16. World Council of Churches, "Alternative Globalization Addressing Peoples and Earth (AGAPE): A Background Document" (Geneva: World Council of Churches, 2005), 20.
17. Capital concentration is evident in patterns of transnational corporate sale and stock ownership. The combined sales of the top 200 transnational corporations is equivalent to over 25 percent of world gross domestic product. One percent of the U.S. population owns 33 percent of all U.S. stock. The next 9 percent own 43 percent. Thus 76 percent of U.S. stock (including that indirectly owned through pension plans) is owned by just 10 percent of the population. See "State of Working America Preview," July 2004, Economic Policy Institute, http://www.epinet.org/newsroom/releases/2004/07/040713-SWAstocks.pdf.
18. AGAPE, 6, 8. On care see Athena Peralta, "A Caring Economy" (Geneva: World Council of Churches, 2005). My discussion of strategies draws on the AGAPE document, particularly 14–22.
19. See http://www.newrules.org/finance/tobin.html and www.currencytax.org for more information on a currency tax. The WCC and other organizations have also called for changes in the voting structures of the World Bank and IMF, with a stronger voice for developing countries. This is very unlikely, particularly with the appointment of Paul Wolfowitz as president of the bank. Russell Mokhiber and Robert Weissman caution: "Everything about Wolfowitz's career, including his time in Indonesia and overseeing Iraqi reconstruction, suggests he is likely to intensify rather than reform the failed World Bank corporate-led model of development." From "The Wolfowitz Coup," posted at http://lists.essential.org/pipermial/corp-focU.S./2005/000201.html.
20. AGAPE, 14.
21. Daryll Ray, Daniel de la Torre Ugarte, and Kelly Tiller, *Rethinking U.S. Agricultural Policy: Changing Course to Secure Farmer Livelihoods Worldwide,* Agricultural Policy Analysis Center, University of Tennessee, September 2003, 2–3.

# Chapter 11

# Ensuring Sustainability

*John B. Cobb Jr.*

I write as a Christian theologian. Does that make any difference in judging what policies our nation should adopt? I think it does. This does not mean that all Christians will come to the same conclusions. Much depends on what we derive from the Bible and make central to our theology. Some of the most vocal Protestants today emphasize a few verses from the Bible about the apocalypse and focus on otherworldly concerns to the detriment of caring about our present crises. Other Christians read the Bible as a book of laws dealing especially with sexuality despite Paul's vigorous denunciation of legalism. They are likely to call for government policies that prescribe their interpretation of morality as the law of the land. Nevertheless, I believe one can say with some objectivity that these are not the main themes of the Bible. Far more faithful to the Bible is an emphasis on God's care for the poor and socially vulnerable. Many Christians across a wide spectrum of Protestants and Catholics, both conservatives and progressives, call for government policies that protect those who cannot protect themselves. I identify myself with this basic understanding of the implications of Christian faith for public policy. But I fear that not all who take this position think it through in sufficient depth. We are called, as Christians, not only to protect the poor and the weak but also to be in solidarity with them, to look at what is happening in the world with an eye toward how it affects the most marginalized among us.

This certainly involves listening to the poor and weak and taking very seriously what we hear. However, it may not entail agreeing with them in their assessments and policy proposals. Those who live from hand to mouth necessarily focus their attention on what is needed so that they can obtain food and shelter for themselves and their families in the immediate future. This short-term orientation can be exploited by the economic and political establishment. It may also be exploited by religious charlatans and the sellers of drugs. Our task as Christians who are not under such immediate economic and psychological pressure is to view matters in a broader context, both with regard to the social order now and the longer term prospects. But it remains our task to view the issues in terms of what happens to the poor. I call this the "bottom-up" perspective.

The bottom-up perspective remains a relatively rare one. It leads to conclusions that are not even considered by most governments. It is at the extreme fringe in most universities. The major media seem hardly aware of it as an alternative. The world is run by those whose perspective is top-down. For those whose perspective is bottom-up, the policies based on top-down thinking are disastrous. Today, a Christian does not view the "bottom" as composed only of poor and vulnerable human beings. The bottom consists in the other creatures with which we share the planet as well as the most vulnerable human beings. To focus on the "bottom" is to view human events in the context of what is happening to the physical planet.

However, one does not have to understand oneself as a Christian in order to adopt this view. Many of those most dedicated to it have given up on the church and take this point of view as self-justifying without reference to God or Christ. Also, one can draw similar conclusions in the context of other religious communities. As a Christian I celebrate the fact that we can think and work together with those who are not Christian. It would be a mistake, however, to minimize the importance of drawing on our traditions and communities in shaping this point of view. Viewing matters in Christian perspective can have revolutionary consequences.

In this chapter I will discuss the global situation in which we find ourselves to illustrate the difference between a Christian bottom-up perspective and the now dominant top-down perspective. When we ask about the global environment we are forced to recognize that, thus far, the policies of the United States are for the most part exacerbating the global problem. This is apparent in multiple ways.

First, we are refusing to participate in global agreements designed to improve the world's chances of avoiding environmental catastrophes. This refusal is most evident in our relation to the Kyoto Accords. While the Clinton administration participated in the formulation of these accords through the work of then Vice

President Al Gore, the United States has since made clear that it does not support them. Now, one may argue (and I would agree) that these accords are flawed in serious ways. These flaws might even be considered sufficiently serious to call for renegotiation of the accords rather than signing them as they are. But the position of the United States has not been to work for improvement. It has been to refuse to enter into any agreement that might hamper the growth of the American economy or the freedom of our corporations.

We could reflect for some time on why the United States adopts an antienvironmental stand when a majority of its people favors moving in the opposite direction. We could then reflect on what political activities might lead to change. It may even be that the most important political strategy is to clarify the vision of what could be. What could be is a national commitment to lead the world in slowing down global warming. This would be in the long-term interest of all the world's people, even if not in the short-term interest of some important corporations. Unfortunately, "long-term" here does not mean a matter of centuries. It is a matter of decades, perhaps only two or three, before global warming is likely to result in critical problems for humankind.

A second way in which U.S. policy exacerbates global problems is through our military power. Our nation has shifted its emphasis from diplomacy to unilateral domination. That is, we declare ourselves free to take those actions needed to establish and maintain our national dominance with or without the support of other nations. This policy requires, of course, having such overwhelming military superiority that no other nation can challenge us. It requires also the willingness to use that power based only on our own judgment.

The environmental consequences are apparent. Building and maintaining a huge military machine requires the massive consumption of scarce resources. When this machine is used, as in Iraq, the consumption escalates, and the destruction and rebuilding also require great quantities of energy. To dominate the whole world requires control of energy sources, especially oil. More and more of this diminishing resource is used for maintaining this control. From an environmental point of view, this escalating use of scarce resources for purposes that do not benefit the world's people is undesirable. The United States should, instead, be leading the world into careful husbanding of resources and directing their use to the places of greatest human need while planning strategies for adjustment as these resources give out.

A third problem of U.S. policy relates to the way in which the United States dominates international economic policy both directly and indirectly (namely, through the Bretton Woods Institutions—the World Bank, International Monetary Fund, and World Trade Organization). The policies that we promote are systematically justified as those that increase global production most rapidly. But the speeding up of global production, unless drastically controlled by environmental considerations, hastens the exhaustion of scarce resources and the worsening of pollution. Without global environmental protection policies, and given that national governments are penalized when they institute such protections, the global deterioration of the environment is inherent in current policy. The approach that we need toward economic policy is to establish a global institution that would ask what kinds of economic activities are environmentally sustainable and then, systematically, develop policies to encourage just those activities.

From an environmental perspective, the United States should reverse most of its global policies. It should support international agreements already reached and lead in developing others. It should shift from the goal of military control of the world to the goal of working with other nations to save the world from environmental disaster. It should shift from promoting economic growth as such, that is, the volume of market activity, regardless of its human and environmental consequences, to promoting a sustainable economy that would meet human needs.

Even if the United States reversed its overall policies from those that hasten the coming of environmental disasters to those that slowed this process, there would be other work to do. The world is in need of imagination! The efforts that now go into researching more sophisticated ways to destroy one another, on the one hand, and to prolong the lives of those who can afford high-tech medical care, on the other, need to be redirected toward such critical matters as finding sustainable ways of producing enough food for the world's people without the use of petroleum products.

At present the only projects of this sort that the government supports are high-tech bioengineering. There is a deep-seated assumption that science and technology can enable us to survive human-caused disasters. From the point of view of the environment, previous "advances" of this sort, such as the "Green Revolution," have done as much harm as good. The Green Revolution developed genetically altered strains of rice and wheat, which were able to absorb more fertilizer and thereby provide larger yields. The requirements of these plants make agriculture far more dependent on oil and irrigation, just when it is clear that oil and fresh water are globally scarce resources. The Green Revolution also intensified the race between the evolution of new pests resistant to poisons and the development of new poisons. While this major "advance" did greatly increase the quantity of grain at a time when such an increase was badly needed, the future of food production is more precarious and vulnerable than ever before. Every indication is that the current solutions of genetic alteration of crops will have similar ambiguous consequences. Biotech "solutions" of this sort are likely to lead to the kind of "overshoot and collapse" of population that occurred with the Irish potato famine. While the introduction of the potato enabled Irish farmers to feed more children, the potato blight ended the population growth and even led to widespread starvation.

From an environmental perspective, a very different kind of imagination is needed. Government policy could well support experiments in quite different directions. First, we need to be absolutely clear about what our current policies are and where they are leading us. Present development policy promotes the "modernization" of agriculture, which means shifting from dependence on natural soil fertility, rainfall, and solar energy to dependence on irrigation and oil-based fertilizers, herbicides, and insecticides. It is a shift from human and animal labor to the extensive use of oil-consuming machinery. The change is also from producing for the local market to the shipment of food over vast distances, transported, of course, by oil-consuming trucks, trains, and ships. There is no doubt that overall this change dramatically raises "productivity," meaning the amount of production divided by the hours of human labor involved. Often, but certainly not always, it also increases total production.

This shift is from a relatively sustainable agriculture to a drastically unsustainable one. In addition to exhausting aquifers and requiring energy for the movement of the water to the places it is needed, irrigation typically reduces fertility by salinization. All the other elements in the modern system are oil-dependent. Yet we know that within a decade or so, if not sooner, the supply of oil will no longer meet the demand. The price will rise, and the market will distribute the oil to those who can pay the higher price. The poor will suffer most, but all economies will be hard-hit as prices of food and all other oil-dependent goods rise dramatically.

The more that people in poor countries have become dependent on modern agriculture, the worse will be the crises that hit them. Sadly, they cannot easily return from modern to traditional modes of farming. The modern farming methods will have destroyed much of the natural fertility of the soil. They will also have led to extensive desertification. In part due to "modernization," traditional practices applied to land not suitable for it, changes in global weather, and rapid population increase, the United Nations predicts that Africa will lose two-thirds of its arable land within twenty years. A crisis of this magnitude is hard to imagine. Would that the United States devoted its research resources to envisioning a positive future for Africa in the midst of these prospects!

Once we are clear about what we are doing and what its consequences will be, we are ready for the second step—seriously considering alternatives. These are possible, and even, in some cases, actual. There is real hope for changes that reverse the direction agriculture has taken in recent decades.

Cuba provides an interesting, and partly encouraging, example. Under Castro Cuba long worked to modernize its agriculture. That meant specializing in what it could produce most advantageously within the global communist market: sugar. It developed large sugar plantations owned and operated by the government. These functioned much the same as agribusiness, using motorized equipment, fertilizer, herbicides, and insecticides, all dependent on oil. It imported oil and food from the Soviet Union in exchange for sugar. Then came the collapse of the Soviet Union and the end of this exchange.

Cuba urgently needed to feed its own people without benefit of oil. The large agribusiness-like monoculture production facilities found the shift to organic food production extremely difficult. Within three years, however, the portion of agriculture still controlled by small farmers succeeded in making the change. Also, urban dwellers produced some of their own food in patches of urban space. Despite great hardship, massive hunger was avoided. Small-scale organic farming can feed Cuba. But Cuba has also shown that the farther a country has gone in the direction of agribusiness monocultures, the more difficult this change will be.

In the United States the Amish have shown that family farming, little dependent on oil, is possible even in the current unfavorable context. Their production per acre is comparable to that of (unsustainable) agribusiness, and it is far more sustainable. It provides a promising model, but its adoption by others will require deep changes in attitude and culture as well as objective practice.

Wes Jackson noted that even Amish agriculture, the best that we now have, gradually erodes the soil. It is not truly sustainable. He established the Land Institute near Salina, Kansas, to develop a truly sustainable agriculture. He noted that the prairie had for millennia produced rich vegetation in a way that actually built up the soil. Once human beings began plowing it, erosion began. The prairie vegetation provided food for numerous animals and included plants that could be eaten by human beings as well. Yet the amount of human food produced was far less than the production of the unsustainable farms that replaced it. What was needed was to find ways to produce far more human food with methods like that of the prairie.

The prairie vegetation was largely perennial, and it was highly diverse. Jackson's goal was to develop a polyculture of perennials that would be as productive as current monocultures of annuals. His work has been to develop strains of perennials that produce far more food and to find the right mixture of them. He set out to accomplish his goal in fifty years. After twenty-five years he thinks he is halfway there. If his project is successful he will demonstrate the possibility of truly sustainable organic food production.

What does this have to do with government policy? It means that all those policies that have systematically depopulated the American countryside and separated the vast majority of Americans from the land should be reversed. There are a few policies already in place encouraging small-scale organic farming. The government could support these much more strongly while discontinuing support for oil-dependent monocultures.

But I am asking for more than that. Jackson has had to do his experimenting without public funding and even against the spirit of government-sponsored projects in schools of agriculture. He has had to spend much of his time raising money from private sources. At best, his work will show what can be done in one climatic region and with one type of soil. But his work in principle is relevant to what is done everywhere. If government policy were oriented to developing an environmentally sustainable system of food production, not only in the United States but also all over the world, it could make money available for this research rather than for that now carried on to improve the profits of agribusiness. That would be an enormous reorientation. It could certainly reduce the suffering that lies ahead and provide for rebuilding on a sustainable basis.

Agriculture is only one area in which we are becoming more and more dependent on oil even when we know that we are running out of it. We are also building our cities in ways that increase our dependence on this soon-to-be exhausted resource. This fact is already attracting some encouraging attention.

At present this takes two main forms. Many are interested in reducing the need for oil in transportation. Efforts have been made to persuade motorists to double up in their use of cars and even to switch from private to public transportation. We already have policies, inadequate though they are, that push for cars that get more miles to the gallon. There are also efforts to find alternative fuels. All of this is certainly to be applauded. As the price of gas rises we may expect increasing public support for such efforts, and that should translate into stronger governmental policies.

We have also had our consciousness raised about how we can be more efficient in the use of oil in our homes. Many of us have solar water heaters on our roofs. Building methods have improved so that there is less loss of warm or cool air through walls and windows and around apertures. We now have more efficient lighting and other electrical appliances, and since much of our electricity is produced by oil, this is also quite directly relevant. On the whole, public policies and building codes have improved in their support of such practices.

Nevertheless, nationally, the use of oil for transportation and buildings has continued to increase. We are a long way from reversing the tide and seriously preparing for the end of the petroleum era. Even if the policies mentioned above are pushed much more strongly, we will not be able to deal with this transition without extensive suffering. If our government would adopt as a major goal researching the possibility of social systems and infrastructures that would not depend on oil, and experimenting with these, the anticipated catastrophes would be significantly delayed and mitigated.

Instead of simply making our use of oil more efficient, desirable as that is, we need to imagine an attractive society that requires very little oil in order to function well. For example, instead of improving motor transportation, we need to envision a city in which there is no need for motor transportation. Of course, it is not enough to imagine such cities; we need to experiment with building them.

We do not have time to rebuild all the existing cities in such ways. This is not a recipe for solving all the problems connected with the end of the petroleum age. We also need research on how the inhabitants of modern cities can survive the lack of petroleum. But the sooner we begin to construct a different kind of city, the longer the crisis can be postponed and the less severe will be the accompanying suffering.

Consider the situation in China. Urban construction there may exceed that of all the rest of the world put together. Currently, China is building cities in a way that is dependent on oil for transportation, heating and cooling, and much else besides. The economic growth of China is one of the reasons that demand on oil supplies will soon be greater than production. One might suppose that it is already too late to do much about this. The die is cast; the construction has already occurred. But this misrepresents the situation. There are still eight hundred million Chinese living in the countryside. The modernization of agriculture will drive hundreds of millions of them into cities. It matters how these new cities are built. My recommendation would be to maintain a labor-intensive agriculture rather than shift to an oil-dependent modern one. But even so, a healthy agricultural system in China does not need the current rural population. Chinese cities will grow.

What would a city be like that was not dependent on oil for its healthy functioning? Fortunately, we already have some imaginative answers. The one to which I have long been drawn is that of Paolo Soleri. He describes his proposed cities as architectural ecologies or "arcologies." Instead of spreading out over large tracts of what is often the best agricultural land, Soleri's arcologies would have a small base. They would achieve their ability to house all urban functions by rising to skyscraper heights. But instead of many skyscrapers, separated by city streets, there would be a single building for the entire city.

Soleri envisions several levels of basement in which manufacturing would take place. The waste heat from the factories would be used to supplement passive solar energy to provide the energy needed in the rest of the arcology. The private dwellings would be located at the outer surface of the building so that they could have direct access to sun and fresh air. Stores, schools, offices, businesses, hotels, parks, entertainment, and everything else would be located in the interior.

Movement within the arcology would be by elevator, escalator, moving sidewalks, bicycling, and walking. These would use a fraction of the space now required for motor transportation within the city. They would also make it possible to go from any part of the city to any other part in a fraction of the time now required in modern cities. In addition, one would never be far from the exits, which would lead directly to exterior parks, farmland, and wilderness. Motor transport might function as horses now do for recreation in the countryside for those who can afford this luxury, but transportation between cities would be public.

I have mentioned passive solar energy. Obviously, how much could be done with this depends on many factors. There are already indications that it is possible to construct large buildings that depend on passive solar energy alone for heating and cooling. Soleri proposes to design arcologies so as to have maximum exposure to the sun in the winter and minimum in the summer. Further, he proposes that an arcology could be built on top of a hill, with the hillsides covered with greenhouses. The air rising through these greenhouses would enter the arcology and provide energy for the factories. At the same time, the greenhouses could provide both employment and food for the inhabitants.

One problem is not solved by this proposal. Arcologies would require lots of natural resources, including oil, in their construction. Whether more or less than today's conventional cities is an open question. If we wait until oil is extremely scarce to begin building in a different way, we may not be able to afford either arcologies or any other kind of city. But this is all the more reason to direct national policy toward envisioning new forms of urban habitat now, while the resources for such experiments are still available.

I have focused in all this on oil and the need to prepare for its scarcity. That is by no means the only reason for drastic change. The need to slow climate change is equally acute. The maintenance of biodiversity is of great importance as well. I could have focused instead on such things as the disappearance of forests, the decline of marine life, the shortage of fresh water, the threat of plagues, or the increase of wars over scarce resources. I have chosen the end of the petroleum era because this is the most widely recognized crisis looming ahead of us. Some believe that price signals from the market are all that will be needed to change individual and social behavior in needed ways. But even they do not deny that major changes will be required.

There may be more chance of the government doing research on how to get through this crisis than on responding to any of the others. In general, genuine response to any one of these crises will reduce the threat of all of them. I can imagine that, if the price of oil doubles rather abruptly a few years from now, a politician might win the presidency on the promise of developing a crash program to reduce national dependence on oil both in the short run and in the long haul. In that case the sorts of efforts I am proposing might be considered.

## QUESTIONS FOR DISCUSSION

1. If oil were to become a scarce commodity in the next ten years, how would your life have to change? What kinds of public policies need to be put in place now to avert potential future crises? What do you think the role of the government ought to be in researching and developing alternative fuel sources?

2. Identify all of the ways you could personally change your lifestyle to use less oil. Cobb goes beyond individual lifestyle changes and proposes small-scale agriculture, nonoil-based transportation, and arcologies. What other examples can you envision that would ensure sustainability? How could you influence your community or congregation to act sustainably?

3. How can we take a "bottom-up" perspective when it comes to the

environment? How do the Bible and the Christian tradition support such a perspective? How might such a Christian perspective have revolutionary consequences?

## RESOURCES

### Books and Articles

Cobb, John B., Jr. *Sustaining the Common Good: A Christian Perspective on the Global Economy.* Cleveland: Pilgrim Press, 1994.

Daly, Herman E. and John B. Cobb Jr. *For the Common Good: Redirecting the Economy toward Community, the Environment, and a Sustainable Future,* 2nd ed. Boston: Beacon, 1994.

Klare, Michael T. *Blood and Oil: The Dangers and Consequences of America's Growing Dependency on Imported Oil.* New York: Metropolitan Books, 2004.

Lerner, Steve. *Earth Summit: Conversations with Architects of an Ecologically Sustainable Future.* Bolinas, CA: Common Knowledge Press, 1991.

Soleri, Paolo. *The Urban Ideal: Conversations with Paolo Soleri.* Ed. John Strohmeier. Berkeley: Berkeley Hills Books, 2001.

### Organizations and Web Sites

Information about Arcology. www.arcology.com.
The Land Institute. www.landinstitute.org.
Union of Concerned Scientists. www.ucsusa.org/global_environment/global_warming/index.cfm.
Cosanti Foundation. www.arcosanti.org.
Renewable Energy. www.renewableenergy.com.
Re-energy. www.re-energy.ca.

### Videos and DVDs

*The End of Suburbia: Oil Depletion and the Collapse of the American Dream.* The Electric Wallpaper Company. 2004.

*Soleri's Cities: Architecture for Planet Earth and Beyond.* Home Vision Entertainment. 1993.

# Chapter 12

# Challenging Our Assumptions

*Mary Elizabeth Hobgood*

In an essay written some years ago, Scripture scholar Walter Brueggemann tells a story about two strangers who have a wordless encounter in a tearoom. The story goes something like this: The first to arrive at the shop is a "very proper" white woman. She orders a pot of tea and retrieves a paper from her bag. She anticipates a leisurely time reading, sipping tea, and eating a small package of cookies she purchased with the paper. As she settles down at a table for two, a "Jamaican black man" comes over and takes the other chair because the shop is quite crowded. As she begins to read, she slips a cookie out of the bag and eats it. Amazingly the man also takes a cookie from the bag. She decides to ignore her astonishment and continues reading. After a while she takes another cookie and so does the man. She can feel her blood pressure rising as she contemplates his unmitigated nerve. While she glares at him, he takes the fifth and last cookie out of the bag and offers her half. At this point she can contain her outrage no longer. She gathers up her things, quickly pays her bill, and leaves the shop in a huff. Outside in the cold she fumbles for bus money. Much to her chagrin she finds a package of unopened cookies in her purse.[1]

This story helps us to see how dominant beliefs can obstruct both our self-knowledge and our ability to respond to others. Brueggemann challenges affluent people, the 20 percent of both the U.S. and global populations that enjoy high salaries and good benefits, to seek a "right reading of social reality, of social power, and of social goods."[2] Otherwise, we, the relatively affluent and mostly white people who read this book, are like the woman in the story who blithely takes what actually belongs to another. It is true that most of "us" are not the *source* of this thievery because we do not live off our assets but work to support our families and ourselves. Even if we are not in the less than 5 percent of the U.S. population that own and control business, however, our participation in varying degrees of affluence as relatively high earners places us in a position to enjoy privilege that does not really belong to us. Therefore, creating justice in our households, communities, and nations requires challenging false assumptions about the nature of reality and our place in it. For, if our assumptions about the world are faulty, they will prevent us from knowing our true situation of privilege. If our worldview is similar to the one probably held by the woman in this story, it will handicap us in the struggle to live justly.

This chapter examines three popularly held but questionable beliefs. The first is that "normal" or "typical" persons are "like us," mostly white and hard-working but able to participate in some modicum of affluence. A second assumption is that affluence and poverty are not structurally related to each other in our political economy, so that people occupy their places in society due to random luck or individual hard work (or lack thereof). The third assumption is that people traditionally called "the poor" are distinct and separate from everyone else and what happens to them will never seep into the lives of the affluent.

My thesis is that unless these assumptions are challenged, we are not likely to realize that *the affluent also have a stake in the struggle for justice.* I believe this knowledge is fundamental if we are to sustain the energy and perseverance necessary to do the work of justice prescribed in this volume. I also suggest three projects to enhance our ability to love our neighbors in the twenty-first century. First, we need education for economic literacy, including an analysis of our own growing vulnerability in the global economy and ravaged ecosphere. Second, we need grassroots political organizations across the United States to help people understand class dynamics, especially who has the power, who owns the goods, and who is eating from the tables of the hungry.[3] Third, we need a movement within the mainline churches that can offer an alternative vision of Christianity to that of the religious right. In contrast to the understanding of many white, conservative, evangelical Christians and some U.S. Roman Catholics, liberation and salvation are about equalizing social power. As Brueggemann notes, justice is about giving back to others what belongs to them even though we have had it so long we think it is ours.[4]

# THE SMALL WORLD MINORITY OF WHITE AFFLUENT PEOPLE

Even though 80 percent of the world's people are living in economic insecurity and various degrees of impoverishment and even though 70 percent are not white, affluent whites have been socialized to think of ourselves as "average" or "typical." In reality, the typical human being is impoverished and comes from one of the many global communities of color. These "world majority people" constitute two-thirds to four-fifths of the world's population, including increasing numbers in the United States.

Most white affluent people, for all our education, often know little to nothing about the typical human being. The vast majority of the world's population suffers deepening economic misery on a daily basis. According to the United Nations' *Human Development Report*, at the end of the twentieth century the richest 20 percent of the global population controlled over 85 percent of total income and wealth. Since then the gap has only widened *between* the affluent and impoverished countries as well as between the affluent and impoverished sectors *within* each of these countries. Workers across the globe, including those in the United States, are in a downward slide, experiencing reduced education, health care, wages and benefits, and limited if any security in retirement. Though most Americans do enjoy relative wealth when compared to the world majority, those of us who still enjoy fairly easy and abundant access to quality education, health care, high wages, and retirement benefits are about 20 percent of the U.S. population, and are hardly the average human being.

# WEALTH CREATES IMPOVERISHMENT

When the affluent, mostly white "world minority" come to understand how power is monopolized through the class structure, we can learn how our own affluence and relative social security is connected to the impoverishment of the overwhelming majority. Two resources in particular may enlighten us as to how the political economy reproduces affluence and impoverishment simultaneously, as two sides of the same coin: critical economic theory and teachings about wealth and impoverishment in the Hebrew Scriptures and the New Testament. Critical economic theory explains why income disparities between and within nations will widen in the current period of capitalism. A liberation reading of Scripture aids us in understanding why this polarization is *the* theological problem for the white affluent minority.

First, critical social theory challenges dominant views of class location as a consequence of culture, personal initiative, and luck. Wealth and impoverishment are not conditions that happen at random to two separate groups. Rather, wealth is created when those who own and control business pay workers less than the value of what they produce. The "surplus value" that workers produce becomes excessive profit for a relatively few investors who have little or no role in the creation of this wealth. Profit also trickles down to high-salaried professionals—CEOs, lawyers, managers, and accountants—who run the corporate system as well as the academics, physicians, and other professionals who serve them. Most workers go along with these conditions because the economically powerful have monopolized the use of land and other resources, including control of education and the media that deprive people of their self-sufficiency and critical understanding. When corporations pay low wages, exploit land, resources, and ecosystems, and use neoliberal economic policies to coerce governments to comply with these arrangements, they create the affluent few and the impoverished majority.

This understanding of impoverishment is found not only in critical economic theory, but also in the Bible—a surprise to many Christians. One of the terms for wealth used by the Hebrew prophets is *plunder* or stolen goods (see Isaiah 3:13–15; Jeremiah 22:13–17; Amos 8:4–6). Many New Testament scholars claim that this understanding of the relationship between wealth and poverty is echoed in the ministry of Jesus, who sees the wealthy as an oppressive social class.[5] Many of the teachings of the Torah, the Hebrew prophets, and Jesus recognize an unjust relationship between wealthy people and economically insecure people. As Beverly Harrison observes, the Scriptures make clear that justice is at the center of Christian life because the struggle for justice reveals the nature of God. Justice is not a matter of charity or giving back a fraction of the plunder, but rather of restoring to our majority sisters and brothers what the political economy has, quite legally, stolen from them.[6]

Most of the relatively few upper-income earners, like the vast majority of workers who earn low wages, sell our labor in order to live and are not the source of class injustice. Nevertheless our salaries allow us some privilege from the surplus value provided by workers below us. It is true that none of us participated in the creation of the economic, racial, and sex-gender systems that constantly reproduce these injustices. Nor are we the source of the problem itself since we do not own and control the big businesses that reproduce the class system. Nevertheless, because we benefit from a political economy that economically exploits, politically oppresses, and culturally marginalizes the majority of the world's people, we are responsible for transforming the structures of power that cause that oppression. *My conviction is that holding ourselves accountable to those who are forced to provide us with "the good life" at their expense is probably the hardest and most important moral challenge to people in the twenty-first century.* Persevering in accountability, as this volume should help us do, is the essential Christian response to social injustice and the rising anger of world majority people.

When we realize how the world majority is forced to live under the intensifying neocolonialism of the current system of globalization, and when we also pay attention to the deepening vulnerability of most ecosystems, we should not be surprised at the growing animosity of people who inhabit a poisoned, plundered, and overdeveloped planet. Indeed, the analytic tools provided by critical economic theory are important for us to acquire not only because of our desire to love our neighbors, but also because when affluent people do not understand the extent of the social and ecological injustice the political economy reproduces, we also put ourselves in great danger. The insight of Martin Luther King Jr., that we will either live together as sisters and brothers or perish together as fools, could not be truer today.

## VULNERABILITY MOVING UP THE CLASS LADDER

It is also a mistake to think that the affluent minority is immune from similar kinds of hardships endured by the world majority. The economic restructuring prompted by globalization has affected formerly high-salaried people who no longer have access to affluent lifestyles and even more people who have lost modest, middle-sector income.

In previous centuries this dynamic of downward pressure on wages used to affect primarily lower-wage earners. In the current stage of capitalism, however, it also affects more and more of those who earn high salaries because corporations are invested in keeping wages low and increasing profits. Consequently, workers in China and India who provide highly educated labor to the U.S. job market are often employed instead of highly skilled, professional U.S. workers. Impoverishment, desperation, and insecurity are the lot of many formerly upper-income workers whose jobs are being downsized, outsourced, mechanized, de-skilled, and de-tenured. In addition, the poisoning of land, air, and water that may serve short-term profits makes even the affluent vulnerable to illnesses we would not otherwise suffer.

Other indicators of the growing peril to the traditionally economically secure include the fact that 40 million Americans work for less than $10 an hour, and half of all single women, many with children, work outside the home in order to scrape by (or not) on $30,000 or less a year.[7] These wages and salaries hardly maintain a so-called middle-class lifestyle in most regions of the United States. Indeed, the gap between rich and poor households more than doubled from 1979 to 2000 and continues to widen.

This economic polarization will only grow worse as corporate logic requires governments and businesses to work hand in glove. Increasingly the political economy functions as one system with a revolving door of shared personnel between business and government. Many people in the United States realize that the most powerful economic interests fund political elections. We are also aware that when politicians leave government, they often move into lucrative jobs with the companies that reward them for legislation that is generous to big business, especially tax breaks, subsidies, and the erosion of environmental laws. Witness, for example, Dick Cheney, who worked for Halliburton, the company awarded the biggest government contracts in rebuilding Iraq, between his stints as defense secretary and vice president. He is only one of a number of politicians whose jobs exist in a revolving door with big business.

In their quest to make unlimited profit for their relatively few investors, many of the largest corporations, especially the banking, communication, and weapons industries, pay increasingly fewer taxes and are dependent on federal subsidies. For example, a study by the Institute on Taxation and Economic Policy found that 275 of the nation's largest corporations paid taxes on, at most, only half their profits from 2001 to 2003, and 46 of these companies paid no federal income tax whatsoever in 2003.[8] Restraints that might hold this drive in check, such as unions, local communities, and national governments, have all been weakened by the growing power of corporations.

Once this fundamental relationship between business and government is understood, it is easy to see why government as currently structured, and elections as currently funded, cannot serve the best interests of the majority of Americans. Most Americans have limited income and own little, if any, corporate stock. With increasingly less means to pay privately for what we need, we should be demanding that government invest in quality public education, health care, and other social welfare institutions, such as secure pensions, upon which our families can rely.

## ECONOMIC AND THEOLOGICAL LITERACY

Understanding economic facts, structures, and relationships helps us see how people who currently sell their labor for middle- and upper-income salaries have more in common with those who make low wages than they do with those in the capitalist class whose income is primarily derived from their ownership and control of the political economy. All workers who must sell labor to live, no matter what their salary or wage, should realize that the profit-making class is invested in getting everyone to work for less.

Widespread economic literacy will take great effort because we have been so thoroughly socialized in U.S. culture to admire and identify with those who are more affluent and to blame those below us on the economic ladder as the source of our problems, especially our economic ones. Most Americans identify themselves as "middle class" and believe that their interests coincide with the interests of the wealthy, a status to which they aspire. We are in great need of developing a class identity that is coherent with our real class position and real economic interests. As upper-income workers our position in the political economy is complex. We are part of a minority that participates in affluence at the expense of the majority. But our economic status is often precarious and we stand to become potentially impoverished by shifts in the global economy and potentially sick due to our ravaged ecosystems. In reality, our interests lie in solidarity with the global majority promoting social change that benefits us all.

Developing class identity is also difficult because many economically insecure people take refuge in social conservatism. Members of right-wing churches, both white, conservative, evangelical Protestants and members of many U.S. Catholic churches, distract themselves from the vulnerability of their shrinking pocketbooks by finding comfort in a conservative social agenda. Seeking explanations for the emptiness of consumerism and the weariness of a 24/7 workweek, they are easily distracted by the "war on terror." Without access to a critical social analysis, people often blame themselves or those less powerful for their economic difficulties. A version of Christianity, bereft of the centrality of social justice, tells them that God will take care of them in all ways, including economically, if they oppose abortion, gay marriage, stem cell research, immigrants, and terrorists. Without the conceptual tools of critical class analysis and lacking access to Christian social justice teachings in Scripture and tradition, conservative Christians are not likely to see how politicians are using the right-wing religious agenda and warmaking to manage peoples' increasing economic, social, and national insecurities.

The manipulation of sexual and economic fears to support right-wing policies will continue as long as people lack knowledge about our social reality, including who has the power and who has the goods. Until intellectual and political struggle deepens, people will remain content with the lowest public attention to the common good of any Western nation. They will identify with those above and blame those below, and believe that funding the wealthy is good because if they work hard enough, they too may be wealthy. They will also continue to believe that publically funded initiatives that support middle-sector and poor people are bad because these people are the losers they are socialized to fear they might become.

## STRATEGIES FOR ACTION

Part of the task of accountability and solidarity requires attention to language because language shapes consciousness and the potential to act in more just ways. I have suggested that those who are white and affluent, even though socialized to believe that we are "typical" humans, should start identifying as the "world minority" or as the "white affluent world minority." My white affluent students tell me that every time they remember that they are, in fact, the world minority and that so-called minorities are actually the world majority, it reminds them to question whose interests are being served by this way of labeling. My lower/working-class white students and students of color tell

me that when they remind themselves that they are part of the world majority, they feel more powerful. They feel less alone in a society that scapegoats
them for its troubles, renders them invisible except for the services they provide others, or celebrates them as tokens that thereby justify the so-called
American Dream.

In the struggle for accountability and solidarity, I suggest we also stop
using the ubiquitous phrase "the poor" in religious discourse. World minority people often speak as if "the poor" refers to a reified, homogeneous category rather than to specific groups among working-class, working-poor, and
unemployed people. Even more dangerously, we project the fallacy that "the
poor" must always exist and will remain a limited constituency. When we say
"the poor," we usually do not think of formerly upper-income chemists or
managers or college-educated people who are losing their homes, flipping
hamburgers for minimum wage, and living in their cars. We believe that the
situations of "the poor" have nothing to do with our own futures in a political economy that is generating vulnerability at the highest rungs of the economic ladder. Given our common reality in a system that is increasingly
denying just entitlements to people who were once privileged, neither charity nor altruism will be sufficient. It is accountability and solidarity that are
faithful to our reality and are the primary characteristics of genuine social justice. Therefore, in place of the term "the poor," I suggest we talk about specific groups of poor people, as well as specific groups of economically
vulnerable people at *all levels* of the capitalist hierarchy.

We also grow in accountability and solidarity when we listen to the working poor and unemployed in our own country and all over the world who are
becoming increasingly vocal in naming what justice requires. What efforts are
we making to discover what they are saying about how we can become their
allies? Most recently, for example, a large sector of two-thirds world nations
under the leadership of Brazil have threatened not to comply with specific regulations of the World Trade Organization (WTO) as long as it allows $300 bil-
lion in annual subsidies to agribusiness in affluent nations. This results in the
cotton, rice, corn, wheat, and soybeans of the wealthy underselling poor farmers and decimating their economies. How can we become allies of two-thirds
world nations whose oil, gas, coal, diamonds, and other minerals become the
source of their poverty when first-world companies plunder them and support
governments that allow this to happen?

In addition to making changes in our own use of language and strengthen-
ing our capacities to listen across class and race divides, I suggested at the beginning of this chapter that we focus on three projects. First, we need to develop
economic literacy to understand why accountability and solidarity are required
of us in light of the class dynamics of evolving capitalism. As I have argued, we
need to develop class identities and help ourselves and others identify the real
reasons for growing economic vulnerability and powerlessness.

Second, we must find ways to reject unjust economic policies, in our nation and globally, especially as they are buttressed by the so-called moral teaching of many U.S. Christian churches. As people of Christian faith, we must be clear that many white, conservative, evangelical Protestants and Catholics have been betrayed by their leaders with regard to the primary content of "moral values" in the Christian tradition. As I have observed, Scripture and tradition are quite clear that economic justice and peacemaking are at the heart of Christian values. Therefore, it is immoral to promote a system of economic injustice and war, to eliminate environmental protections, and to privilege the interests of wealthy individuals and corporations over middle-income and poor families in the United States and abroad. Yet many conservative Christians, both Catholic and Protestant, support unjust policies. As someone from the Catholic tradition, I am saddened when some religious leaders remain silent about the *whole* Catholic tradition, ignoring the teachings on social justice. This only makes it easier for affluent Catholics to vote their pocketbooks while economically struggling Catholics think God supports a conservative social agenda.

My third suggestion is to build grassroots, continent-wide organizations that rival those of the religious right. The religious right has been building a massive organization for over twenty-five years. They are active in every single community across America and now form the base of the Republican Party. The Democratic Party, or any other party for that matter, simply does not have such an infrastructure. Mobilizing four years in advance of an election is not enough. Progressive Christians and class-conscious voters must become as organized as the Christian right. A majority of American Christians needs to achieve some modicum of economic literacy, class identity, and critical Christian consciousness in order to succeed in the kind of social transformation discussed here.

Finally, we must remember that moral intelligence is born in the heart and thus we must probe the links between social and personal transformation. One way of understanding the divinity of Jesus is that he became divine precisely because he became fully human, relating compassionately with sisters and brothers, with earth's creatures, and with the universe itself. However, much of the message of right-wing Christianity stunts our humanity by giving us reasons to exclude others and kill the ecosphere. When our human potential is eroded, so is our ability to connect with others and to live in compassion and justice with all God's creation. We must be critical of reactionary forces within our religious traditions, so that we can struggle more forthrightly against becoming the kind of people this unjust society encourages us to become. What is so troubling to me about the encounter in the tearoom related in the opening story is that it illuminates how affluent people, and yes, even Christian people, are often the unwitting bearers of exploitation and oppression. Our pressing work is to understand the challenges not only of the political economy, but also of our own moral and spiritual integrity.

In taking on a justice-centered agenda for change, the good news is that we can begin to live fuller lives as we rebuild more inclusive, hospitable communities across class, race, sex-gender, national, and religious divides. What a delight to discover that working with others for social justice places us in the company of some of the most generous, courageous, gracious, and interesting people we can ever hope to know! Our work together can witness to the fact that simple and environmentally friendly lifestyles are more carefree and enjoyable than consumer-oriented ones, and that sacrificing greater income for more leisure enhances the quality of life. The friendship and community we can experience with others, when we have more leisure time and when our lifestyles are not built on the suffering of others, will surely bring far more security than consumerism and military spending. We will surely experience greater enjoyment of the goods we do possess when we know our neighbors have what they need.

By implementing the recommendations of the authors in this volume and, even more importantly, by expanding them with our own creative ideas and practices, we can show that it is truly possible for ordinary people to make the political economy more democratic and more just. By our words and deeds, we must relentlessly insist that God's promise of a new creation truly be ours to enjoy.

## QUESTIONS FOR DISCUSSION

1. If you are a member of what Hobgood refers to as the "global minority" of white, affluent persons, how does it change your frame of reference and the way that you think about the world when you shift your orientation to thinking about yourself as part of the world's minority? If you are a member of what Hobgood refers to as the "global majority," how does thinking about yourself in this way change your frame of reference and the way that you think about the world?

2. How might you become more aware of class issues and how might you help educate others in your congregation and community? How might critical class awareness help you organize for change of unjust structures and policies?

3. Hobgood critiques the religious right for ignoring class oppression and poverty and focusing instead on sexual morality and terrorism. How do we uplift concern for social and environmental justice as key moral issues for Christianity, especially in the media? Given that we live in the most religiously diverse country in the world, what role should religion play in developing public policy?

# RESOURCES

## Books and Articles

Brueggemann, Walter. *The Prophetic Imagination.* Minneapolis: Fortress Press, 2000.

Hicks, Douglas A. *Inequality and Christian Ethics.* Cambridge, UK: Cambridge University Press, 2000.

Kadi, Joanna. *Thinking Class: Sketches from a Cultural Worker.* Boston: South End Press, 1996.

Leondar-Wright, Betsy. *Class Matters: Cross-Class Alliance Building for Middle-Class Activists.* Gabriola Island, BC: New Society Publishers, 2005.

Yates, Michael D. *Naming the System: Inequality and Work in the Global Economy.* New York: Monthly Review Press, 2003.

Zweig, Michael. *The Working Class Majority: America's Best Kept Secret.* Ithaca, NY: Cornell University Press, 2000.

## Organizations and Web Sites

United for a Fair Economy. www.faireconomy.org.

Class Action. www.classism.org.

Economic Policy Institute. www.epi.org.

Highlander Research and Education Center. www.highlander.org.

# NOTES

An earlier version of this chapter was a presentation I gave, "Given Global Realities, Who Are My Neighbors?" for The Theological Opportunities Program at Harvard Divinity School on November 11, 2004. I am most grateful to the editors and also to Marvin M. Ellison and Jerry L. Lembcke for suggestions that improved its content and clarity.

1. Walter Brueggemann, "Voices of the Night—Against Justice," in *To Act Justly, Love Tenderly, Walk Humbly: An Agenda for Ministers,* ed. Brueggemann, Sharon Parks, and Thomas H. Groome (Mahwah, NJ: Paulist Press, 1980), 6.
2. Ibid.
3. See, for example, these recent studies of global workers: Michael Zweig, *The Working Class Majority: America's Best Kept Secret* (Ithaca, NY: Cornell University Press, 2000); and Michael D. Yates, *Naming the System: Inequality and Work in the Global Economy* (New York: Monthly Review Press, 2003).
4. Brueggemann, "Voices," 5.
5. Marcus J. Borg, *Jesus in Contemporary Scholarship* (Valley Forge, PA: Trinity Press International), 97–126.
6. Beverly Wildung Harrison, in *Justice in the Making: Feminist Social Ethics,* ed. Elizabeth M. Bounds et al. (Louisville, KY: Westminster John Knox Press, 2004), 16–20.
7. Shannon O'Brien, at the YMCAs of Massachusetts "Money Conference for Women," 9 June 2001.
8. Lynnley Browning, "Study Finds Accelerating Drop in Corporate Taxes," *New York Times,* 23 September 2004, at www.nytimes.com/2004/09/23.

# Index

accessibility, 5, 8, 24
advocacy, 94, 97–98
affluence, 3, 151, 152, 155
affluenza, 41–47 passim
African Association of Earthkeeping Churches, 109
agribusiness, 10, 18–24, 144–46, 157
agriculture, 6, 8, 10, 17–26, 47, 54, 60, 105–10, 127, 143–47
aid, foreign, 33, 102, 131
Alternative Globalization Addressing Peoples and Earth (AGAPE), 134–37
Ambrose, Saint, 104
Amish, 24, 145, 161
Amos, 153
Anzaldua, Gloria, 117–18
arcologies, 147–48
Aristotle, 70, 72

basic needs, 71, 74, 123, 133
Berry, Wendell, 53, 104–05
Bible, themes in, 140, 153
biodiversity, 18, 21–22, 148
biodynamic farming, 19–24
bioengineering, 143
bodies, 54
  caring for, 56–57
Bolivia, 5
Bolton, Herbert Eugene, 116–17
Border Industrialization Plan, 121
borderlands, 12, 116–23
Brazil, 107, 157
Bread for the World, 24, 58
Bretton Woods Institutions, 142
Brock, Rita Nakashima, 35
brownfields, 84, 106
Brueggemann, Walter, 150–51

capitalism, 4–11 passim, 26, 53, 72, 107–08, 128, 152–57 passim
care, 30–32, 37–38, 128–29, 131–34
caregivers, 31–34, 37
Central Intelligence Agency (CIA), 130
China, 4, 21, 128, 147, 154
Christian tradition, 10, 43, 53, 55, 71, 141, 156, 158
church, 9–10, 41–47, 56, 58, 91–99 passim, 107, 121–22, 141, 151, 156, 158
class, 154–55
  identity, 155, 156, 158
Cobb, John, 23
collective work, 82, 84–87
colonias, 120–22
colonization, 108–09
common good, 87
commons, 12, 103–10
communal virtues, 11, 79–82, 86–87
communitarian values, 108
community, 7–10, 22, 55–56, 66–74, 80–88, 92–99, 102–10 passim
community benefit agreements, 67, 69
community development corporation, 95, 100n2
Community Farm Project, 105, 110
community gardens, 47, 106, 110
Community Resources for Responsible Living, 47
community supported agriculture, 10, 17, 23–26, 47, 56, 106–07, 110
compassion, 34–36, 44, 58, 122, 124, 158
complicity, 50, 61n1
consumerism, 73, 122, 156, 129
consumption, 5, 8, 11, 19, 26, 41–47, 51, 59, 127, 133, 135, 142, 161
cooperative, 34, 56, 82

Corinthians, 81, 87
corporate accountability, 67–69, 98
corporate farming, 21, 55
corporate policy, 53, 108
corporations, 5–7, 51, 66–75, 119–21,
    129–31, 135, 142
creation, 12, 42–44, 71, 74, 102–05,
    158–59
Critser, Greg, 52
Cuba, 132, 144–45

Darwin, Charles, 102
debt, 5, 6, 40–41, 46, 108, 131, 133
    cancellation of, 12, 132, 134–36
    social and ecological, 135
deforestation, 109
dehumanization, 122
democracy, 4, 7, 8, 53, 119, 130, 133, 136
deregulation, 4, 128, 134
desertification, 144
Deuteronomy, 100, 133
development
    local, 72, 74, 91–95, 97
    national, 19, 78–79, 128, 132–35,
        142–44
Dillingham Commission, 116
displaced workers, 65–66
domestic labor, 30–37 passim

Earth Charter, 102
earthist, 23, 26
ecology, 105
economic literacy, 151, 155, 157, 158
economic polarization, 117, 154
economics, 4, 6, 36–37, 66, 71, 129,
    152–54
Economy of Communion, 107–08, 110
education, 8, 69, 70, 83, 98, 110, 131,
    135
efficiency, 4, 6, 8, 18–21, 158
Ehrenreich, Barbara, 32
ekklēsia, 2
environmental justice, 8, 78–89 passim
Environmental Protection Agency, 79
ethic
    accountability and solidarity, 157
    land ethic, 73

love, 30, 34–36
    sustainability and biodiversity, 18
eucharist, 55
Exodus, 44, 133
exploitation, 31–32, 37, 42, 76, 93, 158
export-oriented trade, 26

fair trade, 12, 47, 136
faith, 3, 9, 82, 92–93, 119, 121–22,
    127–29, 158
farms, 18–22, 25–26, 54–55, 106–07,
    135–36, 145
farm subsidies, 136
Farm-to-Cafeteria Projects Act, 58
Fernandez, Eleazar, 39n1
Figueroa Corridor Coalition for Economic
    Justice, Los Angeles, 67, 69, 72, 74
First Presbyterian Church of Santa Fe, 106
First Unitarian Church of San José, 47
first world, 25, 32, 151
Focolare Movement, 107–08, 110
food, 1–3, 10–11, 17–27 passim, 33, 46,
    50–59, 73, 94, 105–07, 127, 135,
    141, 143–48
Food Circles Networking Project, 59
Foods Resource Bank, 58
forgiveness, 2–3, 35
free market, 4–6, 72, 107
free trade, 4, 32, 65–66, 133, 135
Free Trade Area of the Americas (FTAA),
    135
Friedman, Thomas, 72
fuel, 19, 22, 44, 46, 51

G-8, 5, 134
General Agreement on Tariffs and Trade
    (GATT), 129
Genesis, 42–44
genetically modified organisms (GMOs),
    52
Ghost Ranch, 106
global capitalism, 11, 34, 53, 72, 107–08
globalization
    alternative, 59–60, 70–75, 133–36
    of housework and child care, 32–34
    neoliberal, 4–7, 18–9, 31–34, 51–3,
        65–7, 78–79, 119–23, 129–33

González Faus, José Ignacio, 122
gospel values, 107, 111
Green Revolution, 19, 143

Harrison, Beverly W., 153
health, 51–53, 109
health care, 1, 5, 8, 74, 84, 128, 131, 135, 152, 155
heart, 10, 25, 31, 33–36, 38, 136, 158
Heifer International, 58
Hillis, David, 101–02
HIV/AIDS, 94–96, 98
Hochschild, Arlie, 32
hope, 9, 11, 44, 81, 121, 136, 144
hospitality, 55, 57–58
household, 9–10, 27, 41, 46, 51–58 passim
household labor, 10–11, 29–38 passim
housing, 1, 69, 94, 96, 98
human dignity, 8, 12, 71, 74
human rights, 32, 130, 135–36
hunger, 3, 22, 24, 53, 58, 136, 145
hybridization, 117

*imago Dei*, 71, 121–22
immigration, 12, 116, 119, 133
impoverishment, 142–54
India, 1, 78, 128, 154
individualism, 8, 71, 122
inequality, 5–7, 12
informal economy, 37–38
instrumental values, 108
interdependence, 10, 23, 25–26, 34, 36, 45
International Monetary Fund (IMF), 5, 19, 66, 127
intrinsic worth, 123
instrumental worth, 123
investment, 4–6, 33, 66, 75, 108, 120, 131, 133–35
Isaiah, 133, 153
Isasi-Díaz, Ada María, 13n1

Jackson, Wes, 145
*jeong*, 31–38 passim
Jeremiah, 153
Jesus, 2–3, 36, 41, 42, 74, 87, 92–93, 109, 122–23, 153, 158
job loss, 4, 93–94, 127

job training, 68, 98
JUBILEE Act, 135
Jubilee movement, 134–36
justice, 7–9, 33–35, 44, 57, 60, 71, 73, 74, 119, 123, 128, 132–34, 151–59 passim
distributive, 119, 126, 131, 133
economic, 6, 31, 37, 67, 70, 71, 136, 158
social, 2, 12, 81, 91, 156–59

Karenga, Maulana, 82, 86
kin-dom, 3, 13n1, 36
King Jr., Martin Luther, 80, 81, 154
Korten, David, 66
Kwanzaa, 82
Kyoto Accords, 141

land, 18–26 passim, 73, 75, 103–110, 130, 133, 140–47 passim
Land Institute, 145
language, 32, 81, 102, 117, 119, 156–57
Latina/o, 188, 121
Laughlin, Harry, 116
legalism, 140
Leopold, Aldo, 73
Leviticus, 133
liberalization, 4, 128, 134, 136
living wage, 8, 32, 37, 68, 74
local hiring, 68, 74
love, 30, 31, 34–36, 38, 57, 74, 80–81, 96, 107, 110, 121, 154
Luke, Gospel of, 36, 133

*maquiladora,* 121–23
Mark, Gospel of, 92
market, 4–6, 21–27, 32, 56, 107–08, 135, 143–44, 148
market expansion, 132
mass movements, 110
McFague, Sallie, 3, 74
Medical Assistance Program International, 94
*mestizaje,* 117–18
Mexico, 4, 12, 21, 65–67, 73, 94, 116–17, 120–23
migrants, 12, 32, 73

military power, 142
mission, 57, 92, 95–96, 98
Mitchell, Harold, 83, 86, 88
monocropping, 19, 21, 24
morality, 105, 140
mutuality, 10, 33–36

national interest, 130
native peoples, 115
Nehemiah, 83, 86–87
neoliberalism, 4, 128
nonprofit organizations, 69, 84, 87, 92, 96–98, 100n8
nonviolence, 80
norm, 31, 43, 44, 70
North American Free Trade Agreement (NAFTA), 4, 65, 133

obesity, 25, 50–58 passim
odious debt, 132
oppression, 8, 9, 13, 31, 35, 93, 153, 158
organic farming, 10, 20, 23, 145
Ousley United Methodist Church in Lithonia, Georgia, 94
overconsumption, 41–45

Paul, apostle, 81, 87
Perkins, John, 130–31
personal responsibility, 108
pesticides, 18–20, 24, 46, 52, 106
place, 8, 43, 72–75, 109, 117, 121
Plato, 70, 102
population, 8, 9, 14, 43, 143–44
poverty, 31, 54, 79, 93, 119–23, 128, 132–34, 151, 153, 157
power, 4–5, 33–34, 66, 70–72, 93, 129, 132, 142, 151–56
principle, moral or ethical, 8, 58, 71, 82, 91, 96, 107
privatization, 4–5, 127–28, 134
productivity, 8, 19, 21, 52, 144
profit, 6–8, 22–23, 53, 67, 70, 72, 123, 134–35, 153, 155
Psalms, 105–7
public policy, 4, 9–10, 26, 67–68, 140
public subsidy, 70
purpose, 9, 82–83, 86–88

race, 33, 35–36, 79, 119, 157, 159
Regenesis Environmental Justice Partnership, 84
regulation, 5, 12
relationality, 29–38 passim
religion, 23, 74, 92, 102, 105, 117
religious right, 151, 158
responsibility, 2, 3, 8, 12, 32, 43–44, 53, 57, 68, 74, 82, 85–88, 108
restitution, 133, 135
Roman Catholics, 115, 118, 151
Romans, Paul's Letter to, 83
rootedness, 11, 70, 72–74
Rural Center for Responsible Living, 23

Sabbath-Jubilee tradition, 133
salvation, 151
Schweiker, William, 123
science, 6, 102, 143
Scripture, 42–43, 82, 86, 93, 152, 153, 156
sexual harassment, 121
simple living, 108
Slow Food movement, 20, 25–27
Smith, Adam, 129
solar energy, 144, 147
Soleri, Paolo, 147
solidarity, 12, 35, 58, 71–75, 123–24, 133, 136, 141, 156–57
spirituality, 3, 11, 60, 107–08, 110, 128, 136
stewardship, 43–44, 47, 91
Strategic Actions for a Just Economy, 69
strategies
    for promoting capitalism and economic integration, 4–7
    for promoting just and healthy societies, 9–12, 36–38
    public policy, 67, 74–75
structural adjustment policies, 5–6, 19, 127–28, 131, 138n2
subsidiarity, 8
subsistence agriculture, 26, 108
sufficiency, 11, 44, 108
sustainability, 6–8, 11–12, 18–20, 43–44, 54, 71

Tabb, William, 128

taxes, 70, 155
technology, 8, 18, 33, 42, 58, 94, 105, 108, 143
Tejanos, 116, 119
Templo Calvario in Santa Ana, 93
theology, 42, 43, 109, 140
third world, 26, 32, 34, 117–18, 129
third-world debt crisis, 131
transformation, 9, 18, 44, 47, 93, 134, 136, 158
transnational corporations, 7, 21, 66, 120, 123, 129–30, 135, 139n17
transnationalization of labor, 31, 72
transportation, 46, 84, 94, 146–48
tree of life, 102–03
two-thirds world, 19, 157

unions, 67, 155
*United Nations Human Development Report,* 6, 122, 152
United States, policies of, 4, 54, 115, 129, 132–36, 141–46
  borderlands with Mexico, 116–18, 123
unity, 82, 86–88, 119
utilitarianism, 104, 110

values, 6, 19, 23, 52, 53, 59, 71, 91, 107, 108, 117, 122, 123, 128, 133, 158

volunteering, 25
vulnerability, 35–36, 91, 133, 151, 154, 156–57

wage, just, 121
war on terror, 13n4, 156
wealth, 4, 6–7, 41, 108, 119, 130–32, 139n17, 152–53
women, 29–37, 121, 128, 154
work, 6–11, 65–66, 74–75, 120–21, 123, 134, 151
  collective, 82–88
  domestic, 29–38
World Bank, 5, 7, 12, 19, 26, 66, 127–35, 142
World Council of Churches (WCC), 128
world majority people, 152–54
world minority people, 157
World Trade Organization (WTO), 5, 66, 129, 142, 157

Young, Iris Marion, 72

Zimbabwean Institute of Religious Research and Ecological Conservation, 109
Zion Hill Baptist Church in Atlanta, 95